A book of

Lexical Resource
Word Power is the World Power

Rajesh Sheth
(S. Raja)

Published in India

First Printing, 2020

E-book: ASIN: B08RB6BTDR

Paperback: ISBN:

Gunjan Prakashan
Pallavi Towers
Navarangpura,
Ahmedabad, India 380009

The woods are lovely, dark and deep,
But I have promises to keep,
And miles to go before I sleep,
And miles to go before I sleep.

- Robert Frost

This Book Belongs to...

A gift from ....

Date: .... Place: ....

Contents

Section 1

Section 2

This first book is dedicated to...

Dear Pappaji and Mummiji...

You were expert readers and writers...
Your suggestions
made me read good books
made me write letters
made me listen to good music
made me speak along with all......
So,
I imagined
I thought
I pondered
I visualized
I mused.....I understood.
And now,
I write...
I recite...
I render...
I articulate...
I create...
I define...

This first book is dedicated to you.....

And, a lot of thanks to...

My wife Bhakti, my son Chintan, and my daughter Radhika.
And, my siblings, Jitubhai, Kiranben, Divya, as well...
And my niece and nephews, Bittoo, Adit, Dhanu and Parth, also...

You inspired...
You poked...
You praised...
You admired...
You liked...
You patronized...
In a nutshell, you all boosted confidence in me.

All my works are yours...

Acknowledgement

I owe my gratitude to:

Linda Stanton French, the daughter of a well-known American author and humourist, Will Stanton, who has stretched her helping hand by reviewing and pointing out all the places of corrections. For several years, she helped get her father's short stories and articles, ready for submission, to editors, posthumously prepared his last novel for publication, and worked in the field of publishing. She has a great deal of experience in the writing and publishing fields.

My friend, **Wing Commander, Nilesh Gandhi** needs special mention towards pointing out my silly yet serious blunders that only a Veteran could have noticed!!!

An author and a friend, **Mr. Jagdeep Dhebar** (JD Sir) aka Jasper Dell, for his incessant inspiration to bring about this piece of literary essence under your worthy eyes. He is an author.

Mukesh Raval, a math genius, who put a great trust in me to be in front of his hundred of students. He has been my friend philosopher and guide since 2009. My taught are either engineers or doctors or successful entrepreneurs, today.

Parth Sheth, my nephew, who literary pocked me to come up with a nice publication. He is an upcoming music composer who got training at KMMC, Chennai.

Meshwa Creation, Ahmedabad, for the process of designing and page formatting, and exercising their rich experience earned as a senior designers in the town.

A few organizers of English Language Classes for supporting me at all the stages of this first publication, *Lexical Resource*. Not only that, a few students have always been with me to accomplish this mammoth task.

All who have inspired me directly or indirectly and have put trust and faith in me. This publication is just a petal of the flower, several petals are yet to follow from the garden of enduring task.

Rajesh Sheth (S. Raja)
Author and Writer
Cambridge English Trainer

Lexical Resource

Foreword

It has been observed that the English Language is an integral part of many citizens' lives all over the world - it has become the essential second language. Many students, when they pursue masters or higher education at universities around the world, need to prove their proficiency in the English language. This need provoked Rajesh to create a book of lexical resource.

Rajesh has now taught Cambridge English to two generations of students in India. Having known and observed many non-native English-speaking students, he came to a conclusion that test takers needed to have a better command of grammar and vocabulary. So, during his teaching profession, he created a multitude of notes and study materials with a view to augmenting the language skills of his students. These notes have been edited over and over and have formed the shape of his new book, LEXICAL RESOURCE.

This book's goal is to boost the vocabulary of students in effective ways; teaching them to find, study, and use more descriptive words that will make their sentences more interesting and colorful, while also making the meaning of their writing more specific and accurate.

Proficiency in word building and the usage of a good lexical resource is a must for all test takers of foreign language who seek certification in that language. That importance is the focus of this book. All test takers of English in non-English-speaking countries should refer this publication by Rajesh Sheth (S. Raja). His compilation will have great value to them.

Linda Stanton French
Maryland, USA

Lexical Resource

Preface

The ever-increasing importance of expected performance (Bands or Points) in the English proficiency tests has insisted and urged me to create and publish this book of Lexical Resource.

An examiner will always look at your range, choice and accuracy of vocabulary, and see how well your words help you to express your thoughts. **Lexical Resource** is evaluated in Writing and Speaking Tasks. These two tasks are productive skills. Developing these skills through **Lexical Resource** is much useful.

To achieve a desired high score, one needs to show a wide range of vocabulary and sentence structure. This concise content of Lexical Resource in this set of three books that is thoroughly imagined, compiled, and collected from different most reliable sources. The content is then corrected, written freshly, and presented in a practical and easy manner for you.

This book, **Lexical Resource,** is exclusively prepared after long face to face meetings with inquisitive students. These learners, like you, have always been eager to improvise their Writing Skills by using the immense wealth of Lexical Resources.

I have been inspired by my students to present this collection before you. I thank all the students who have followed the footprints of my teachings and guidance.

Rajesh Sheth
Ahmedabad

Lexical Resource

About the Book

      This book of **Lexical Resource** is a must read for all test takers of English language. Lexical knowledge is knowledge that can be expressed in words.
A vast knowledge of vocabulary (Word Power) is nothing but reference of Lexical Resource. The enhancement of your rich vocabulary through these three books of **Lexical Resource** shall boost your score. In general, the wider the range of words or expression employed appropriately and suitably, the better the score will be.

      This first part of **Lexical Resource** shall help you to have a reference of variety of words that shall come through your learning process. Word choice is an important task while writing or speaking so that you can impress your examiner or reader or listener. Many words are supported with synonyms and the nearest meanings.

Key features:

- Basic understanding of Collocation/Less Common Words/Paraphrasing/ Synonyms/Connotation
- Abstract nouns with synonyms and the nearest words
- Qualifying words with collocation (Adjectives + related Noun)
- Variant and thematic range of Adjectives
- Degree of Adjectives
- Traits (Positive, Negative and Neutral)
- The Royal order of Adjectives

Remember, this is not a 'Dictionary' but a reference book to find out selected words.

Lexical Resource & IELTS

Are you taking IELTS?

This information is vital for you while you are taking the IELTS test. With a view to getting a good desired score of either 5.5 or 6 or 6.5 or higher in the IELTS, one must achieve all the **criteria** in a balanced manner.

What are these criteria?

Four criteria are quintessential in any English test: Task. Out of four criteria, Lexical Resource is one of the criterion. An examiner assesses the score on a variety of words and idiomatic expressions used, which should be without any repetition. These are meant for Writing and Speaking Tasks.

TAR: Task Achievement and Task Response
CC: Coherence and Cohesion
LR: Lexical Resource
GRA: Grammatical Range and Accuracy

How to manage these skills?

Topics of TAR and **CC** are covered in forthcoming book **Lexical Resource Part 3.**
LR is well understood in this book **'A Book of Lexical Resource' Part 1.**
Always remember, **Word power is the World power.**
GRA is made understood in the forthcoming book, *'Grammar Made Easy'.*

How to use this book...

Always read the instructions and follow the rules. All the specified examples are for you to make supplementary examples.

- This book is not for mere reading only.
- Work with the content, the words, the examples.
- Read them aloud...Write them once...
- Make your own new sentences...
- Send those sentences as messages to your friends...
- Revise them..

Along with your reading through eyes and using mind, use a pencil or a pen and a notebook to write them. Active participation with the book shall allow you to enhance the power of words. To boost up more knowledge, use a few online dictionaries to understand in detail. Follow the same without ignoring them. A few tips are given in all the units.

Salient Points to Ponder:

- Understand the Lexical Resource
- Synonyms are for references and usages
- Collocation is understood by Adjectives + Nouns
- Paraphrasing is understood by similar words or phrases
- Connotation must not be confused with Synonyms
- Never use common words and expression
- Try to find uncommon expression of a common word

Abbreviations:

N = Noun   Adj. = Adjective   V = Verb   Adv. = Adverb

Lexical Resource

A range of vocabulary is focused on in this criterion. A candidate should use a wide range of words and expressions correctly to score high. Using a variety of words and interpretations, one shall get a higher score and shall stand tall in a group. Proficiency in the language is identified by good grammar, appropriate lexical resources, and confidence. Lexical Resource denotes and includes a few essential factors or prerequisites to fulfill. Now, let's understand a few criteria. These are as follows:

1. **Collocation:**

Collocation is a way of expression of using two words together that makes a real meaning. It can't be learned by rules. It takes a time of practice for the user to master collocation. One should be aware of the turn of the phrase.

Example:

V + N ...Make some food/ Do some work/ Commit some crime

Adj + N...Fewer people/Dense forest/Amazing story

V + Adv...Speak slowly/Run quickly/Write swiftly

Adv +Adj...Quite sure/Reasonably cheap/Seriously injured

Adj + Pre...Nice of/Kind to/Sorry for/married to

2. **Less common words or terminology.**

One should use uncommon words at times. Using **idiomatic expressions** or colloquial or verbal phrases to improvise the meaning.

Examples:

- Good words can be food for thought.

- I can't stand his attitude. He is impossible.

- My mother runs an extra mile to earn money.

- Let's go through the topic again.

3. Paraphrasing:

Paraphrase is the interpretation of some words or expressions in other words without changing the meaning. It is used when we want to re-state something with fewer words. On not finding any word, one must not stop writing or speaking but should use other similar expressions. Usually, synonyms are used to fulfill this criterion.

- I need to sit in *an air-conditioned room.*

  I need to sit in *a cool place.*

- They are *my uncle's children.*

  They are *my cousins.*

4. Synonyms:

Words are used with similar or nearest meanings when used. Synonyms help us to choose wide range of vocabulary.

- The word 'Speak' is 'Say'.

- 'Important' can be 'Essential'.

- 'Smart' can be 'Clever'.

- 'Beauty ' can be 'loveliness'.

- 'Ability' can be 'Aptitude'.

5. Connotation:

When any word or expression is rephrased by using another similar expression, we mean it **Connotation**. It is also important that real meanings or the cultural values are not lost and are presented in a suggestive metaphorical way. It can be referred to as **Metaphor** also.

- He is such a dog. (His behavior is like a dog.)

- He acts childish. (It is a foolish act.)

So, work hard and start your journey of Words and Words and Words…

Section 1:
Nouns are Nouns

We use some words for a person, place, thing, situation, feeling, subject, or an animal. Grammatically, these names are nouns.

Countable and uncountable nouns are the major two types of nouns. A noun that we can count is 'a countable' and one that we can't count but can measure is 'an uncountable' noun.

Say...

A man:	A person	(Countable)
Mr. Sheth:	Surname of a person	(Uncountable)
Rajesh:	Name of a person	(Uncountable)
City:	A place	(Countable)
Bangalore:	Name of a city	(Uncountable)
Happiness:	Feeling (not a thing)	(Uncountable)
Wood:	Material	(Uncountable)
Mobile:	A thing	(Countable)
Rhinoceros:	An animal	(Countable)
Software:	An abstract noun (not a thing)	(Uncountable)

Chapter 1:
Nouns Always singular
(Uncountable)

Abstract Nouns :

Points to ponder:

> ➢ These beautiful words are not concrete, but we can feel and experience them. In other words we can't see or touch them.
> ➢ Usually, we need, want, give, take, seek, lose, share and have these abstract nouns..
> ➢ We can derive these words either from Verbs or Adjectives. Example: Speak (V) becomes Speech (N)
> ➢ These words are usually singular but, sometimes, used as plural at places according to usage.

These almost 1250 words define the...

- Status
- Condition
- Concept
- Idea
- State
- Form
- Stage
- Event
- Circumstance
- Nature

- Behavior
- Feeling
- Emotion
- Sentiment
- Mood
- Situation
- Stage
- Action noun
- Measurement
- Way...

Function of Abstract Nouns:

These abstract nouns are widely positioned in sentence construction when we want to limit the usage of adjectives and verbs. They are also used to avoid repetition of words. A good sentence is always balanced with verbs, adjectives, adverbs and these Abstract Nouns.

Using abstract nouns in a Paraphrase: It is important to understand 'Paraphrase' in IELTS while task completion of Reading, listening, Speaking and Writing. Paraphrase is the use of different words to convey the same idea. Questions in listening and reading will have the paraphrased answer. Here we have used similar abstract nouns in two sentences.

Examples:
* **He has vast ability to accomplish the task.**
* **He has vast capability to complete the job given.**

By Nominalization: Using a word from the word family

While completing a reading task you will come through a situation when the question words will be different than the words in the reading portion.

* Text part: Many **people** were too **weak to walk**.
* Question part: **Weakness/lack of strength** of **the citizens** hindered their **mobility**.

You can mark that similar words are used in question part... Now, try to find the answer. Whether the question statement is true or false or not given.

It becomes easy to use Abstract Nouns as they are uncountable and don't need any article! Isn't it easy?

Some important study tips:
The list contains a few synonyms and some nearest words.
One should use these given words wisely!!!
(Don't Copy..Understand and use as per the usage)
A few words are noun & verb both, so they have been identified as (n & v)

A vast collection of 'Abstract Nouns':

1. **Ability**
   - aptitude
   - skill
   - capability
   - capacity
2. **Adolescence**
   - teenage years
   - teens
   - youth
   - puberty
3. **Adoration**
   - love
   - esteem
   - high regard
   - respect
4. **Adventure**
   - escapade
   - jaunt
   - experience
   - quest
5. **Advice**
   - recommendation
   - suggestion
   - guidance
   - opinion
6. **Admiration**
   - value
   - reverence
   - worth
   - esteem

7. **Amazement**
   - astonishment
   - wonder
   - admiration
   - surprise
8. **Anger**
   - annoyance
   - irritation
   - fury
   - rage
9. **Annoyance**
   - irritation
   - exasperation
   - vexation
   - indignation
10. **Anxiety**
    - nervousness
    - worry
    - concern
    - unease
11. **Artistry**
    - creativity
    - originality
    - imagination
    - adeptness
12. **Audacity**
    - daring
    - boldness
    - courage
    - cheek

13. **Authority**
    o power
    o jurisdiction
    o dominion
    o dominance
14. **Awe**
    o fearfulness
    o wonderment
    o astonishment
    o dread
15. **Awkwardness**
    o clumsiness
    o ineptness
    o inelegance
    o discomfort
16. **Beauty**
    o loveliness
    o attractiveness
    o prettiness
    o exquisiteness
17. **Belief**
    o faith
    o conviction
    o confidence
    o trust
18. **Benevolence**
    o generosity
    o compassion
    o munificence
    o kindness
19. **Birth**
    o delivery
    o confinement
    o beginning
    o labor
20. **Bravery**
    o courage
    o valor
    o gallantry
    o daring

21. **Brilliance**
    o brightness
    o intensity
    o vividness
    o luster
22. **Brutality**
    o cruelty
    o viciousness
    o violence
    o rough treatment
23. **Calmness**
    o tranquility
    o serenity
    o quietness
    o peace
24. **Catastrophe**
    o disaster
    o calamity
    o upheaval
    o devastation
25. **Chaos**
    o disorder
    o confusion
    o bedlam
    o pandemonium
26. **Charisma**
    o charm
    o captivation
    o appeal
    o magnetism
27. **Charity**
    o help
    o aid
    o offerings
    o donation
28. **Clarity**
    o clearness
    o lucidity
    o simplicity
    o precision

29. **Charm (n & v)**
    o attraction
    o magnetism
    o allure
    o amulet
30. **Coldness**
    o chilliness
    o detachment
    o dispassion
    o frigidity
31. **Comfort (n & v)**
    o ease
    o calmness
    o reassurance
    o relief
32. **Communication**
    o transmission
    o imparting
    o conveying
    o reporting
33. **Compassion**
    o sympathy
    o empathy
    o consideration
    o kindness
34. **Complaint**
    o grievance
    o criticism
    o protest
    o grumble
35. **Confidence**
    o complacence
    o aplomb
    o assurance
    o self-reliance
36. **Consideration**
    o thought
    o deliberation
    o reflection
    o contemplation

37. **Contentment**
    o satisfaction
    o happiness
    o pleasure
    o gratification
38. **Contribution**
    o donation
    o input
    o involvement
    o bequest
39. **Control (n & v)**
    o management
    o dominance
    o authority
    o power
40. **Courage**
    o bravery
    o guts
    o audacity
    o fortitude
41. **Creativity**
    o originality
    o imagination
    o inspiration
    o ingenuity
42. **Crime**
    o offense
    o wrong
    o felony
    o misdeed
43. **Culture (n & v)**
    o civilization
    o society
    o traditions
    o customs
44. **Curiosity**
    o inquisitiveness
    o curiousness
    o nosiness
    o snooping

45. **Danger**
    - hazard
    - risk
    - peril
    - threat
46. **Dare (n & v)**
    - challenge
    - audacity
    - boldness
    - cheek
47. **Darkness**
    - night
    - dusk
    - gloom
    - obscurity
48. **Dawn (n & v)**
    - sunrise
    - beginning
    - commencement
    - daybreak
49. **Death**
    - demise
    - doom
    - loss
    - fatality
50. **Deceit**
    - dishonesty
    - treachery
    - deception
    - deceitfulness
51. **Dedication**
    - devotion
    - commitment
    - enthusiasm
    - keenness
52. **Defeat (n & v)**
    - beat
    - overcome
    - overpower
    - surmount

53. **Defense (n & v)**
    - protection
    - resistance
    - guard
    - security
54. **Definition**
    - delineation
    - depiction
    - distinction
    - explanation
55. **Delight**
    - enjoyment
    - pleasure
    - happiness
    - delectation
56. **Demise**
    - end
    - finish
    - decease
    - doom
57. **Democracy**
    - equality
    - egalitarianism
    - social equality
    - republic
58. **Desire (n & v)**
    - wish
    - want
    - longing
    - craving
59. **Despair**
    - misery
    - desolation
    - hopelessness
    - anguish
60. **Destruction**
    - obliteration
    - annihilation
    - devastation
    - demolition

61. **Determination**
   - will-power
   - fortitude
   - grit
   - strength of mind
62. **Dexterity**
   - deftness
   - adroitness
   - handiness
   - agility
63. **Dictatorship**
   - tyranny
   - autocracy
   - despotism
   - totalitarianism
64. **Difference**
   - dissimilarity
   - disparity
   - distinction
   - divergence
65. **Dimness**
   - softness
   - faintness
   - gloom
   - gloominess
66. **Disappointment**
   - dissatisfaction
   - displeasure
   - distress
   - discontent
67. **Disbelief**
   - incredulity
   - doubt
   - distrust
   - skepticism
68. **Disparity**
   - inequality
   - inconsistency
   - discrepancy
   - gap

69. **Disquiet**
   - unrest
   - uneasiness
   - worry
   - anxiety
70. **Distraction**
   - bafflement
   - disruption
   - diversion
   - confusion
71. **Distribution**
   - allocation
   - allotment
   - supply
   - sharing
72. **Disturbance**
   - trouble
   - commotion
   - riot
   - uproar
73. **Diversion**
   - distraction
   - change
   - deflection
   - detour
74. **Division**
   - separation
   - splitting up
   - bifurcation
   - partition
75. **Domination**
   - control
   - authority
   - command
   - supremacy
76. **Donation**
   - bequest
   - endowment
   - gift
   - contribution

77. **Dreams (n & v)**
    o vision
    o illusion
    o delusions
    o fancy
78. **Education**
    o teaching
    o learning
    o schooling
    o tutoring
79. **Ego**
    o self-respect
    o self-image
    o pride
    o self-esteem
80. **Elegance**
    o stylishness
    o grace
    o modishness
    o sophistication
81. **Embarrassment**
    o discomfiture
    o awkwardness
    o humiliation
    o mortification
82. **Employment**
    o occupation
    o work
    o labor
    o vocation
83. **Encouragement**
    o support
    o back-up
    o boost-up
    o incentive
84. **Endearment**
    o allurement
    o sweet talk
    o beguilement
    o loving words

85. **Endorsement**
    o backing
    o support
    o approval
    o sanction
86. **Endurance**
    o patience
    o stamina
    o fortitude
    o strength
87. **Energy**
    o power
    o force
    o vigor
    o liveliness
88. **Enhancement**
    o improvement
    o augmentation
    o development
    o enrichment
89. **Engagement**
    o rendezvous
    o commitment
    o betrothal
    o date
90. **Enthusiasm**
    o eagerness
    o interest
    o keenness
    o ardor
91. **Envy (n & v)**
    o jealousy
    o greed
    o desire
    o resentment
92. **Evil**
    o wickedness
    o malevolence
    o sin
    o iniquity

93. **Examination**
   - assessment
   - test
   - evaluation
   - reviewing
94. **Excitement**
   - enthusiasm
   - thrill
   - elation
   - delight
95. **Fact**
   - detail
   - reality
   - actuality
   - authenticity
96. **Faculty**
   - talent
   - ability
   - power
   - aptitude
97. **Failure**
   - breakdown
   - stoppage
   - malfunction
   - collapse
98. **Faith**
   - confidence
   - trust
   - reliance
   - assurance
99. **Faithfulness**
   - authenticity
   - realism
   - closeness
   - accuracy
100. **Faithlessness**
   - infidelity
   - inconstancy
   - fickleness
   - betrayal

101. **Fascination**
   - charm
   - attraction
   - appeal
   - interest
102. **Fatality**
   - loss
   - casualty
   - death
   - doom
103. **Favoritism**
   - preference
   - partiality
   - nepotism
   - penchant
104. **Fear (n & v)**
   - terror
   - dread
   - horror
   - fright
105. **Fitness**
   - health
   - strength
   - robustness
   - vigor
106. **Forgiveness**
   - amnesty
   - clemency
   - absolution
   - mercy
107. **Fragility**
   - weakness
   - frailty
   - feebleness
   - tenderness
108. **Frailty**
   - imperfection
   - shortcoming
   - defenselessness
   - ill-health

109. Freedom
- liberty
- autonomy
- independence
- liberation

110. Friendship
- companionship
- amity
- acquaintance
- comradeship

111. Generosity
- kindness
- bigheartedness
- openhandedness
- bounty

112. Goodness
- decency
- kindness
- honesty
- integrity

113. Gossip (n & v)
- rumor
- hearsay
- tittle-tattle
- scandal

114. Grace (n & v)
- elegance
- refinement
- loveliness
- polish

115. Graciousness
- courteousness
- politeness
- civility
- sociability

116. Greatness
- magnitude
- enormity
- immensity
- vastness

117. Grief
- sorrow
- heartache
- anguish
- angst

118. Guidance
- leadership
- direction
- supervision
- management

119. Guts
- bravery
- courage
- daring
- fortitude

120. Happiness
- contentment
- pleasure
- gladness
- cheerfulness

121. Hate (n & v)
- abhorrence
- detestation
- hatred
- odium

122. Hatred
- extreme dislike
- disgust
- revulsion
- loathing

123. Hazard
- danger
- peril
- risk
- vulnerability

124. Help (n & v)
- assistance
- lending a hand
- aid
- facilitation

Lexical Resource

125. **Helpfulness**
- kindness
- neighborliness
- goodwill
- concern

126. **Helplessness**
- defenselessness
- passivity
- blatancy
- vulnerability

127. **Honesty**
- sincerity
- truthfulness
- integrity
- frankness

128. **Honor (n & v)**
- respect
- admiration
- credit
- reputation

129. **Hope (n & v)**
- expectation
- optimism
- anticipation
- wish

130. **Humility**
- humbleness
- modesty
- meekness
- shyness

131. **Humor (n & v)**
- comedy
- wit
- funniness
- the funny side

132. **Hurt (n & v)**
- harm
- injure
- wound
- damage

133. **Idea**
- thought
- design
- plan
- initiative

134. **Idiosyncrasy**
- peculiarity
- eccentricity
- quirk
- habit

135. **Imagination**
- mind's eye
- revelation
- visualization
- thoughts

136. **Impression**
- feeling
- idea
- notion
- thought

137. **Improvement**
- development
- upgrading
- enhancement
- advancement

138. **Infatuation**
- obsession
- craze
- passion
- fascination

139. **Inflation (economics)**
- price rise
- intensification
- escalation
- augmentation

140. **Information**
- details
- knowledge
- news
- notification

141. **Insanity**
    o madness
    o lunacy
    o psychosis
    o mental illness

142. **Integrity**
    o honesty
    o truth
    o truthfulness
    o reliability

143. **Intelligence**
    o cleverness
    o aptitude
    o intellect
    o astuteness

144. **Invention**
    o creation
    o discovery
    o development
    o innovation

145. **Investment**
    o asset
    o speculation
    o savings
    o venture

146. **Jealousy**
    o envy
    o covetousness
    o suspicion
    o distrust

147. **Joy**
    o delight
    o happiness
    o pleasure
    o Joy

148. **Justice**
    o fairness
    o righteousness
    o a fair chance
    o coreectness

149. **Kindness**
    o compassion
    o sympathy
    o gentleness
    o kindheartedness

150. **Knowledge**
    o information
    o literacy
    o familiarity
    o wisdom

151. **Laughter**
    o amusement
    o hilarity
    o mirth
    o delight

152. **Law**
    o rule
    o commandment
    o regulation
    o decree

153. **Liberty**
    o freedom
    o independence
    o autonomy
    o emancipation

154. **Life**
    o existence
    o biography
    o longevity
    o verve

155. **Loss**
    o defeat
    o thrashing
    o hammering
    o failure

156. **Love (n & v)**
    o affection
    o adoration
    o worship
    o esteem

157. **Loyalty**
   o faithfulness
   o devotion
   o trustworthiness
   o allegiance

158. **Luck**
   o fortune
   o chance
   o fate
   o destiny

159. **Luxury**
   o lavishness
   o sumptuousness
   o comfort
   o opulence

160. **Management**
   o organization
   o running
   o administration
   o supervision

161. **Maturity**
   o adulthood
   o prime of life
   o middle age
   o mellowness

162. **Memory**
   o reminiscence
   o recollection
   o recall
   o remembrance

163. **Mercy**
   o compassion
   o pity
   o clemency
   o forgiveness

164. **Misery**
   o unhappiness
   o depression
   o gloom
   o sadness

165. **Motivation**
   o inspiration
   o drive
   o stimulus
   o enthusiasm

166. **Movement**
   o progress
   o mobility
   o faction
   o advancement

167. **Music**
   o melody
   o tune
   o harmony
   o composition

168. **Need (n & v)**
   o requirement
   o obligation
   o commitment
   o necessity

169. **Nostalgia**
   o homesickness
   o reminiscence
   o wistfulness
   o longing

170. **Omen**
   o sign
   o portent
   o prophecy
   o forecast

171. **Opinion**
   o view
   o estimation
   o belief
   o judgment

172. **Opportunity**
   o chance
   o occasion
   o opening
   o break

173. **Optimism**
- hopefulness
- positiveness
- sanguinity
- confidence

174. **Pain (n & v)**
- ache
- hurt
- soreness
- sting

175. **Panic**
- apprehension
- terror
- anxiety
- horror

176. **Parenthood**
- fatherhood
- motherhood
- fatherliness
- paternity

177. **Patience**
- endurance
- tolerance
- persistence
- fortitude

178. **Patriotism**
- partisanship
- jingoism
- nationalism
- devotion

179. **Peace (n & v)**
- tranquility
- silence
- harmony
- serenity

180. **Peculiarity**
- custom
- oddness
- idiosyncrasy
- oddity

181. **Perseverance**
- insistence
- importance
- firmness
- determination

182. **Pleasure (n & v)**
- enjoyment
- happiness
- delight
- bliss

183. **Poverty**
- scarcity
- shortage
- lack
- paucity

184. **Power (n & v)**
- authority
- control
- influence
- supremacy

185. **Pride**
- satisfaction
- self-importance
- delight
- smugness

186. **Principle**
- code
- standard
- belief
- attitude

187. **Property**
- possessions
- belongings
- goods
- assets

188. **Proficiency**
- skill
- ability
- talent
- expertise

189. Quality
- excellence
- superiority
- class
- eminence

190. Radiance
- warmth
- glow
- sparkle
- vivacity

191. Reality
- realism
- actuality
- authenticity
- truth

192. Redemption
- salvation
- deliverance
- emancipation
- escape

193. Redundancy
- circumlocution
- diffuseness
- diffusion
- wordiness

194. Refreshment
- rejuvenation
- stimulant
- bounce
- energizer

195. Relaxation
- recreation
- leisure
- repose
- restfulness

196. Relief
- solace
- comfort
- consolation
- cheer

197. Restriction
- limit
- constraint
- restraint
- ceiling

198. Riches
- resources
- treasures
- reserves
- assets

199. Romance (n & v)
- relation
- love
- feel affection
- adore

200. Rumor
- gossip
- chitchat
- tale
- buzz

201. Sadness
- grief
- sorrow
- unhappiness
- misery

202. Sanity
- wisdom
- understanding
- judgment
- good sense

203. Satisfaction
- agreement
- contentment
- fulfillment
- pleasure

204. Self-control
- self-discipline
- discipline
- restraint
- continence

205. **Sensitivity**
- sympathy
- feeling
- warmth
- compassion

206. **Service (n & v)**
- examination
- tune-up
- examine
- overhaul

207. **Shock (n & v)**
- distress
- surprise
- astonishment
- fright

208. **Siesta**
- rest
- catnap
- forty winks
- midday sleep

209. **Silliness**
- stupidity
- ridiculousness
- childishness
- madness

210. **Sincerity**
- genuineness
- honesty
- seriousness
- earnestness

211. **Skill (n & v)**
- ability
- cleverness
- cunning
- dexterity

212. **Slavery**
- bondage
- enslavement
- servitude
- servility

213. **Sleep (n & v)**
- slumber
- nap
- snooze
- doze

214. **Sophistication**
- style
- classiness
- superiority
- erudition

215. **Sorrow**
- grief
- mourning
- sadness
- distress

216. **Sparkle (n & v)**
- shine
- glitter
- glisten
- twinkle

217. **Speculation**
- conjecture
- gossip
- assumption
- guesswork

218. **Splendor**
- magnificence
- finery
- grandeur
- majesty

219. **Strength**
- power
- might
- potency
- muscle

220. **Strictness**
- severity
- firmness
- sternness
- harshness

221. **Stupidity**
- o foolishness
- o foolhardiness
- o idiocy
- o inanity

222. **Submission**
- o obedience
- o compliance
- o capitulation
- o surrender

223. **Success**
- o achievement
- o accomplishment
- o victory
- o triumph

224. **Support (n & v)**
- o brace
- o buttress
- o mount
- o reinforcement

225. **Surprise (n & v)**
- o revelation
- o disclosure
- o shocker
- o astonishment

226. **Sympathy**
- o understanding
- o compassion
- o kindness
- o consideration

227. **Talent**
- o aptitude
- o flair
- o capacity
- o faculty

228. **Teaching (n & v)**
- o education
- o lessons
- o instruction
- o coaching

229. **Thought**
- o consideration
- o contemplation
- o thinking
- o deliberation

230. **Thrill (n & v)**
- o excitement
- o adventure
- o delight
- o ecstasy

231. **Tiredness**
- o weariness
- o sleepiness
- o fatigue
- o drowsiness

232. **Togetherness**
- o kinship
- o solidarity
- o companionship
- o camaraderie

233. **Tolerance**
- o patience
- o compliance
- o lenience
- o acceptance

234. **Trait**
- o mannerism
- o peculiarity
- o attribute
- o characteristic

235. **Trust (n & v)**
- o faith
- o belief
- o hope
- o conviction

236. **Truth**
- o fact
- o reality
- o certainty
- o accuracy

237. Uncertainty
- doubt
- indecision
- hesitation
- vagueness

238. Understanding (n & v)
- sympathy
- consideration
- thought
- deliberation

239. Unemployment
- joblessness
- being without a job
- job loss
- idleness

240. Unreality
- futility
- emptiness
- uselessness
- pointlessness

241. Venture (n & v)
- adventure
- enterprise
- undertaking
- speculation

242. Victory
- conquest
- triumph
- win
- success

243. Wariness
- caution
- suspicion
- circumspection
- guardedness

244. Warmth
- light heat
- warmness
- tenderness
- compassion

245. Warmness
- heat
- warmth
- graciousness
- reassurance

246. Weakness
- fault
- weak spot
- fragility
- limitation

247. Wealth
- riches
- prosperity
- affluence
- means

248. Weariness
- tiredness
- exhaustion
- fatigue
- lethargy

Tips to Remember:
- A few words are nouns and verbs both, so they have been identified as (n & v).
- Use these words daily in your sentences to memorise and earn a higher score in the criterion of Lexical Resource.

249. **Work (n & v)**
- o labor
- o employment
- o job
- o vocation

250. **Worry (n & v)**
- o fret
- o be concerned
- o agonize
- o concern

251. **Worship (n & v)**
- o adoration
- o love
- o reverence
- o respect

252. **Wrath**
- o anger
- o rage
- o fury
- o annoyance

253. **Yearning**
- o desire
- o longing
- o yen
- o hunger

254. **Yell (n & v)**
- o scream
- o shriek
- o bellow
- o howl

Can you find a few abstract nouns from this drawing?
This is drawn by my daughter.

Material Nouns:

Material nouns are either material or natural things. These things are singular and uncountable.

- **We refer to these words as a mass (a quantity).**
- **The quantifiers such as any, some, a little or much are used to show the quantity of material noun.**

  - We need much oxygen to live.
  - People should use little a *ghee* while cooking.

- **These nouns should be coupled with its container, quantity or measurement.**

  - Please add **a pinch of salt** in the dish.
  - **A cup of tea** is enough for breakfast.
  - **A full bag of wheat** was donated.
  - **A bottle of wine** is nice.
  - **A slice of bread**
  - **A can of petrol**
  - **A spoonful of sugar**
  - **A piece of chocolate**

Material nouns include…

- Metals: Gold, Silver…
- Gases: Oxygen, Perfume…
- Powders: Talcum, Chilly…
- Crystals: Sugar, Salt…
- Jelly: Jam, Squash…
- Food: Bread, *Khichdi*…
- Pulp: Mango pulp
- Paste: Mayonnaise, Cheese

- Slurry: Molasses, Mud…
- Liquid: Water, Petrol…
- Grains: Wheat, Rice…
- Fibers: Cotton, Jute…
- Mass: Lava, Snow…
- Dust: Pollution, Smog
- Nuts: Cashew, Almonds
- Beverage: Tea, Coffee…

A few Examples of Material Nouns:

1. Acrylic
2. Agar-agar
3. Alcohol
4. Aluminum
5. Barley
6. Beer
7. Bread
8. Butter
9. Buttermilk
10. Cement
11. Chalk
12. Cheese
13. Chicory
14. Chilly
15. Chocolate
16. Coal
17. Coco
18. Coffee
19. Cotton
20. Cream
21. Curry
22. Diesel
23. Drug
24. Earth
25. Electricity
26. Flour
27. Fog
28. *Ghee*
29. Gin
30. Glass
31. Gold
32. Hair
33. Honey
34. Ice
35. Ink
36. Iron
37. Jam
38. Jelly
39. Jute
40. Kerosene
41. Leather
42. Juice
43. Milk
44. Nylon
45. Oil
46. Oxygen
47. Paper
48. Perfume
49. Petrol
50. Plastic
51. Powder
52. Rice
53. Rubber
54. Salt
55. Sand
56. Sauce
57. Scent
58. Silk
59. Silver
60. Snow
61. Soap
62. Soup
63. Squash
64. Steel
65. Sugar
66. Tea
67. Turmeric
68. Water
69. Wheat
70. Whisky
71. Wine
72. Wood
73. Wool
74. Yogurt

Other Miscellaneous Nouns: Things, Observation and Senses

The following examples are always singular and uncountable…And, try to find the nearest words to these to enhance your vocabulary skill.

1. Ambiance
2. Atmosphere
3. Baggage
4. Bonus
5. Clay
6. Climate
7. Clothing
8. Current
9. Cutlery
10. Din
11. Drapery
12. Dust
13. Electricity
14. Equipment
15. Fog
16. Furniture
17. Hair
18. Hearing
19. Homework
20. Housework
21. Incentive
22. Kettle
23. Land
24. Light
25. Lightening
26. Listening
27. Luggage
28. Machinery
29. News
30. Noise
31. Poetry
32. Pollution
33. Rubbish
34. Scene
35. Scenery
36. Sheep
37. Sight
38. Smell
39. Smog
40. Smoke
41. Software
42. Soil
43. Sound
44. Stationery
45. Surf
46. Texture
47. Time
48. Touch
49. Traffic
50. Vista
51. Vision
52. Weather

Correction Tip:
- **Where is my luggage? (not 'luggages')**
- **The furniture in this room is from China. (not 'furnitures')**
- **What is the news? (not 'what are the news')**

Chapter 2:
Nouns
Singular & Plural
(both)

Collective Nouns

Some singular nouns are often used as Plural nouns and take plural verb. These nouns are all groups of people. The plural form indicates many people of that noun. Please mark the different usage in the UK and the US.

For example:

Government:	The government (they) **want** to pass a new law. (UK)
	The government **wants** to pass a new law. (US)
Staff:	The staff (people) at the new office **are** happy. (UK)
	The staff **is** given new task. (US)
Team:	Our team (players) **work** hard to win the match. (UK)
	That team **works** hard to win the match. (US)
Family:	A family **is** going on a tour.
Audience:	The audience **was** happy in the concert.
Committee:	The committee **approves** the new demand.
	The committee **are** arriving.
Company:	A company **holds** the power.
Firm:	The firm **gets** success.
Police:	The police have come.
	A policeman **is** here.
India:	India **have** won the world Cup.
	India (a team of players) **is** playing the final match.

Now, try to make sentences of the following words. These are collective nouns of the group of people/ animals/birds/ things.

1. Squad :   A small group of military people
2. Band: A group of musicians
3. Panel: A group of people who discuss a public topic
4. Board: A group of people with managerial powers
5. Commission: A group of persons directed to perform some duty
6. Parliament: The supreme legislative body
7. Class: A group of students that get together to study
8. Bench :   A group of jury or Judges
9. Gang :   A group of thieves or criminals
10. Crowd :   A group of general mass
11. Mob :   A group of agitated people
12. Crew :   A group of people that manages ship or an airplane
13. Troop :   A group of soldiers
14. Regiment :   A big group of military personal (many battalions)
15. Army :   A very big mass of armed forces on land
16. Brigade :   A large body of troops
17. Fleet: A number of ships under a single command
18. Convoy: A protecting group (specially ships)
19. Throng: A large crowd
20. Horde: A people or tribe of nomadic life
21. Pack: A group of same kind of animals
22. Flock: A group of animals gathered together
23. Herd: A large group of animals kept under human control
24. Society: a community of people having common traditions
25. Swarm: A group of insects (bees, flies)
26. Shoal: A group of fish
27. Staff: People as employee
28. Troupe: A group of dancers
29. Choir: A group of singers
30. Orchestra: A group of musicians (instrument players)
31. Library: A collection of books
32. Colony: A group of people or species having common culture
33. Society: A community of people having common traditions

The following nouns are always in plural-form but usually stated as singular and sometimes, plural .

1. Alms
2. Amends
3. Annals
4. Archives
5. Arms
6. Arrears
7. Belonging/s
8. Billiards
9. Cave/s (n & v)
10. Chaos
11. Chattel/s
12. Clothes (n & v)
13. Compensation/s
14. Condolences
15. Congratulations
16. Contents
17. Looks
18. Curds
19. Damages
20. Draughts
21. Droppings
22. Drugs (n & v)
23. Earnings
24. Eaves
25. Electronics
26. Environs
27. Funds
28. Goods
29. Greens
30. Guts
31. Innings
32. Jitters
33. Mathematics
34. Measles
35. Mumps
36. News
37. Nuptials
38. Oats
39. Obsequies
40. Odds
41. Outskirts
42. Pains
43. Physics
44. Possessions
45. Premises
46. Proceeds
47. Regards
48. Resources
49. Respects
50. Riches
51. Rickets
52. Savings
53. Stairs
54. Surroundings
55. Teens
56. Thanks
57. Tidings
58. Troops
59. Valuables
60. Wages

Examples:
- The funds given to this school are not enough.
- Nowadays, teens are very smart.

Teaser: Have you tried to find other nearest words of the above words?

Other routine items or things are addressed as 'always plural'.

<table>
<tr><td colspan="2">Garments:</td><td colspan="2">Tools:</td></tr>
<tr><td>1.</td><td>Bloomers</td><td>1.</td><td>Bellows</td></tr>
<tr><td>2.</td><td>Breeches</td><td>2.</td><td>Binoculars</td></tr>
<tr><td>3.</td><td>Braces</td><td>3.</td><td>Clippers</td></tr>
<tr><td>4.</td><td>Flannels</td><td>4.</td><td>Cutters</td></tr>
<tr><td>5.</td><td>Jeans</td><td>5.</td><td>Glasses</td></tr>
<tr><td>6.</td><td>Pants</td><td>6.</td><td>Irons</td></tr>
<tr><td>7.</td><td>Suspenders</td><td>7.</td><td>Pincers</td></tr>
<tr><td>8.</td><td>Braces</td><td>8.</td><td>Pliers</td></tr>
<tr><td>9.</td><td>Pantaloons</td><td>9.</td><td>Scales</td></tr>
<tr><td>10.</td><td>Tights</td><td>10.</td><td>Scissors</td></tr>
<tr><td>11.</td><td>Flannels</td><td>11.</td><td>Spectacles</td></tr>
<tr><td>12.</td><td>Pajamas</td><td>12.</td><td>Tongs</td></tr>
<tr><td>13.</td><td>Trousers</td><td>13.</td><td>Tweezers</td></tr>
</table>

Examples:
- Can I take these scissors?
- Where are my spectacles?
- These tights are loose!

More words like these words are in the forth coming book........
The Words and Words and Words

A Note:
Here, we come to a partial conclusion of the chapter of Nouns. The detailed understanding of Nouns is at 'Grammar Made Easy' by S. Raja.

Now let us understand Adjectives in the next section. Always remember that you must use at least one adjective (a qualifying word) before a noun. It can be a number, color, quantity or quality, but use it.

Section 2:
Adjectives

What are Adjectives?

An understanding...

Adjectives: The Words that show Qualities of nouns/names

Adjectives usually describe or modify nouns and pronouns. The qualifying words are of all kinds: colossal, black, happy, extreme, each, special, rare, etc.

Adjectives are also considered as qualifiers and modifiers.

These words define the quality, quantity, number, size, amount, color, taste, looks, appearance, origin, age, condition, situation, and make.

Adjectives are usually positioned before the adjacent nouns; however, sometimes they are placed after verbs as a predicate.

One can change the perception as per usage.

Example:

- This is an **accomplished task.**
- The **task is accomplished**.

An Amazing Fact: (A word family)

These adjectives can be transformed into Adverbs and Nouns!!

Happy(adjective)...Happily(adverb)...Happiness (noun)...

Formation of adjectives:

These adjectives are usually identified by the suffix such as:

1. **-able/-ible**   understandable, capable, readable, incredible
2. **-al/-ial/-ical** mathematical, functional, influential, chemical
3. **-ful**   beautiful, bashful, helpful, harmful
4. **-ic**   artistic, manic, rustic, terrific
5. **-ive**   submissive, intuitive, inventive, attractive
6. **-less**   sleeveless, hopeless, groundless, restless
7. **-ous**   gorgeous, dangerous, adventurous, fabulous
8. **-ent/-ant**   important, independent, variant, magnificent
9. **-an/-ian**   human, agrarian, Spartan, veteran, simian
10. **-y**   fancy, hungry, sleepy, angry, balmy, lengthy
11. **-ish**   childish, selfish, bookish, Spanish, babyish, lavish

Many words with –ing and –ed or –et or V3 (verb in the perfect form) forms are also used as adjectives.

1. Interesting
2. Surprising
3. Deafening
4. Boring
5. Tiring
6. Embarrassing
7. Confusing
8. Disappointing
9. Learned
10. Decided
11. Accomplished
12. Amused
13. Understood
14. Exciting

Points to Ponder:
Please read and mark carefully, in the next page, that a few suffixes of words have been marked bold. These suffixes represent different forms of adjectives. Isn't it amazing to remember!!!!

Collocation of adjectives:

What is Collocation of Adjectives?

Collocation allows the appropriate combination of two grammatical words, an adjective, and a noun so that a clear meaning is achieved.

Collocation is done in such a way that when some words are used together they sound natural together. It means a particular adjective should be used to qualify a specific noun.

For example:

- We should say it was **heavy rain,** or **light rain,**

  (Not, **strong rain or mild rain)**

- Doctor replaced an **injured limb with an artificial limb**.

  (Not, **a false or fake limb)**

- The students should wear a **casual dress**.

  (Not, a **common dress)**

- I am afraid of a **dead body.**

  (Not, a deadly body)

This kind of usage in the language is called **collocation**. There is no clear rule but we should be aware of actual usage. Some words just sound right together, while others do not.

In the next pages, we shall discuss a few positive and negative adjectives with appropriate nouns as collocation. The nouns listed in the second column are mostly used with the adjectives in the first column.

Chapter 1: Positive adjectives

Now, pay attention. The second column shows nouns. These nouns or names are usually supported by the adjectives given in the first column.

Adjective	Related Noun
1. Accomplish**ed**	task/assignment
2. Adapt**able**	situation/ rules
3. Ador**able**	personality
4. Affectio**nate**	nature/person
5. Agree**able**	idea/notion
6. Alert	person
7. Allur**ing**	personality
8. Ambit**ious**	person
9. Ami**able**	nature/person
10. Amus**ed**	person
11. Attent**ive**	person
12. Bound**less**	bounty/limit
13. Brave	person/heart
14. Breathtak**ing**	scene/scenery
15. Bright	day/future
16. Buoy**ant**	time/person
17. Calm	nature/person
18. Cap**able**	person
19. Charm**ing**	personality
20. Cheer**ful**	nature/person
21. Cheery	nature/person
22. Clever	person
23. Coher**ent**	ideas/thoughts
24. Comfort**able**	place/situation
25. Compl**iant**	student/result
26. Conc**ise**	text/ideas/news
27. Confid**ent**	person/nature
28. Considerate	personality/behavior
29. Consistent	progress/result

Adjective	Related Noun
30. Cooperative	person/society/team
31. Costly	affair/thing
32. Courageous	act/person/decision
33. Crazy	behavior/person
34. Credible	act/action/deed
35. Cultured	family/attitude
36. Curious	mind/person
37. Dashing	personality
38. Dazzling	personality
39. Debonair	personality
40. Decisive	point/idea/act
41. Decorous	behavior
42. Delightful	event/thing/place
43. Detailed	information/news
44. Determined	nature/person
45. Diligent	nature/person
46. Discreet	decision/action
47. Dynamic	personality
48. Eager	mind/child
49. Economical	cost/thing/offer
50. Efficient	person/worker
51. Elated	mind/person
52. Eminent	personality
53. Enchanting	place/thing/song
54. Encouraging	attitude/nature
55. Endurable	attitude/task
56. Energetic	person/individual
57. Entertaining	act/scene/person
58. Enthusiastic	person/performance
59. Excellent	result/outcome/
60. Excited	person/being/someone
61. Exclusive	offer/time/proposal
62. Exuberant	person/one/thing
63. Fabulous	offer/place/thing
64. Fair	talk/price/person/decision
65. Faithful	person/animal

Lexical Resource

Adjective	Related Noun
66. Fantastic	idea/place/thing/sight
67. Fearless	person/personality
68. Fine	situation/time/health
69. Frank	opinion/discussion/person
70. Friendly	terms/behavior
71. Funny	act/action/behavior/person
72. Generous	act/person
73. Gentle	person/attitude
74. Gifted	child/person
75. Glorious	moments/time/face
76. Good	person/idea/place
77. Gorgeous	personality/place/scene
78. Happy	moment/person/
79. Harmonious	time/music/behavior
80. Helpful	person/attitude/approach
81. Hilarious	act/moment/story
82. Honorable	person/personality
83. Impartial	decision/choice/verdict
84. Industrious	nature/character/quality
85. Instinctive	quality/skill/trait
86. Intellectual	mind/brain/ person
87. Jolly	nature/person
88. Joyous	moment/time
89. Kind	person/act/nature
90. Kind-hearted	person
91. Knowledgeable	person
92. Likeable	thing/person
93. Lively	person/moment/animal
94. Lovely	person/time/ thing
95. Loving	nature/act/behavior
96. Lucky	person/one
97. Mature	person
98. Modern	time/thing
99. Nice	being/stage/situation/status
100. Obedient	student/child/one
101. Painstaking	moment/time/thought

Adjective	Related Noun
102. Peaceful	situation/time/period
103. Perfect	work/decision/picture
104. Placid	water/place/time/nature
105. Plausible	rate/price/act
106. Pleasant	place/time/character/temperament
107. Pleased	personality/moment
108. Pleasing	personality/time/conduct
109. Pleasurable	decision/thing/moment/time
110. Plucky	one/person/character
111. Productive	idea/ decision/work
112. Protective	person/ situation/thing
113. Proud	person/moment
114. Prudent	individual/act/decision
115. Punctual	person
116. Quiet	moment/time/place
117. Receptive	terms/conditions/ nature
118. Reflective	thought/ideas
119. Reliable	person/one
120. Relieved	situation/person
121. Resolute	attitude/approach/manner
122. Responsible	person/
123. Rhetorical	name/word/idea
124. Righteous	values/decision/verdict
125. Romantic	person/situation/place
126. Sedative	drug/medicine/treatment
127. Seemly	situation/thing
128. Selective	attitude/act/behavior
129. Self-assured	person/human being/one
130. Sensitive	person
131. Shrewd	person
132. Sincere	act/action/attitude/person
133. Skilful	act/person
134. Smiling	person/statue/picture
135. Splendid	place/result/outcome/
136. Steadfast	decision/act/person
137. Stimulating	idea/thought/time/thing

Adjective	Related Noun
138. Striving	nature/lecture/person
139. Sturdy	nature/body/physique
140. Successful	person/work
141. Succinct	discussion/conversation/chat
142. Talented	person/personality
143. Tempting	situation/thing/offer
144. Thoughtful	act/person/decision
145. Thrifty	person/attitude
146. Thriving	future/development
147. Tough	situation/time
148. Tranquil	moments/place/time
149. Trustworthy	person/organization
150. Unbiased	decision/verdict/judgment
151. Unlimited	offer/time/food
152. Unusual	situation/offer/position
153. Upbeat	attitude/nature
154. Valiant	soldier/warrior/act
155. Vigorous	exercise/act/work
156. Vital	advise/decision/ information
157. Vivacious	temperament/ action/ person
158. Warm	feelings/approach/atmosphere
159. Watchful	act/action/person
160. Willing	person/nature
161. Wise	person/act/decision
162. Witty	personality/nature/act/behavior
163. Wonderful	scene/place/thing/idea
164. Zealous	person/act

Examples:
1. **A willing person** is always successful.
2. Yes, definitely, this is a **wise act.**
3. We are going to have a **thriving future**.
4. That boxer has **sturdy physique**.
5. We like his **pleasing personality**.

A note: Please refer to a good dictionary for meanings of these adjectives.

Chapter 2: Negative adjectives

Here, are a few negative adjectives with synonyms and possible related nouns. We can make use of a few more nearest related words of negative adjectives. Note that a few adjectives have (N) after the word. It denotes that it can be a neutral adjective as well.

Negative adjectives	Related Nouns

1. **Abrasive**   surface/texture/nature
    - rough
    - coarse
    - harsh
    - rasping
2. **Abrupt**   idea/sentence/act
    - sudden
    - unpredictable
    - immediate
    - quick
3. **Abusive**   talk/behavior
    - rude
    - insulting
    - offensive
    - obnoxious
4. **Afraid**   animal/child
    - frightened
    - scared
    - fearful
    - terrified
5. **Aloof**   identity/person
    - distant
    - detached
    - unfriendly
    - cold

Negative adjectives	Related Nouns
6. Ambiguous	idea/statement
• vague	
• unclear	
• uncertain	
• confusing	
7. Angry	person/individual
• annoyed	
• irritated	
• fuming	
• irate	
8. Anxious (N)	student/person
• apprehensive	
• nervous	
• worried	
• uneasy	
9. Arrogant	attitude/person
• conceited	
• haughty	
• egotistical	
• bigheaded	
10. Ashamed	person
• embarrassed	
• shamefaced	
• mortified	
• humiliated	
11. Awful	thing/time/situation
• dreadful	
• terrible	
• appalling	
• calamitous	
12. Bad	feeling/time/person
• shocking	
• ghastly	
• dire	
• unpleasant	

Negative adjectives	Related Nouns

13. Belligerent   person/discussion
- aggressive
- argumentative
- quarrelsome
- confrontational

14. Bewildered   person/situation
- confused
- puzzled
- dazed
- befuddled

15. Boorish   manner/actions
- rude
- ill-mannered
- impolite
- rough

16. Bored   person/talks
- uninterested
- fed up
- listless
- jaded

17. Boring   thing/book/time
- uninteresting
- tedious
- dull
- dreary

18. Callous   person/time/action
- heartless
- unfeeling
- coldhearted
- uncaring

19. Careless   act/attitude/person
- slapdash
- hasty
- casual
- sloppy

Lexical Resource

Negative adjectives	Related Nouns
20. Clumsy	idea/situation/time
• awkward	
• inept	
• ungainly	
• gauche	
21. Combative	action/attitude
• argumentative	
• antagonistic	
• aggressive	
• belligerent	
22. Confused	person/being/situation
• puzzled	
• perplexed	
• baffled	
• mystified	
23. Cowardly	act/action/deed
• gutless	
• spineless	
• weak	
• craven	
24. Crazy (N)	person/idea/situation
• wild	
• passionate	
• fanatical	
• extreme	
25. Creepy	situation/time
• sinister	
• frightening	
• eerie	
• scary	
26. Cruel	person/action
• unkind	
• mean	
• nasty	
• brutal	

Negative adjectives	Related Nouns
27. **Cynical**	person/activities/tricks

- pessimistic
- mocking
- sarcastic
- distrustful

28. **Dangerous**	deeds/situation/place/person

- unsafe
- hazardous
- risky
- perilous

29. **Daunting**	person/nature/attitude

- intimidating
- off-putting
- discouraging
- scary

30. **Deceitful**	person/deed

- dishonest
- deceiving
- fraudulent
- untrustworthy

31. **Defeated**	team/country

- beaten
- overcome
- conquered
- whitewashed

32. **Defective**	thing/item/article

- faulty
- imperfect
- flawed
- out of order

33. **Defiant**	person/personality

- disobedient
- insolent
- insubordinate
- rebellious

Lexical Resource

Negative adjectives	Related Nouns

34. **Depressed**   person/heart
- miserable
- unhappy
- down in the dumps
- dejected

35. **Deranged**   ideas/task/person
- unbalanced
- unhinged
- disturbed
- mad

36. **Disagreeable**   ideas/suggestions
- unpleasant
- distasteful
- offensive
- nasty

37. **Disillusioned**   person/one
- disenchanted
- disappointed
- disheartened
- cynical

38. **Disturbed**   person/one
- troubled
- bothered
- concerned
- distressed

39. **Domineering**   attitude/person
- bossy
- dominant
- overbearing
- officious

40. **Draconian**   law/rule/commandment
- harsh
- strict
- extreme
- drastic

Negative adjectives	Related Nouns

41. **Embarrassed**   one/person
   - mortified
   - humiliated
   - gauche
   - uncomfortable

42. **Envious**   feelings/speech/person
   - jealous
   - covetous
   - green with envy
   - resentful

43. **Erratic**   attitude/behavior/one
   - unpredictable
   - inconsistent
   - inconsistent
   - irregular

44. **Evasive**   idea/talk/thoughts
   - elusive
   - slippery
   - shifty
   - cagey

45. **Evil**   person/soul
   - wicked
   - malevolent
   - sinful
   - errant

46. **Faded**   thing/item/idea
   - gray
   - dull
   - washed out
   - pale

47. **Fanatical**   one/attitude/behavior
   - obsessive
   - dedicated
   - fervent
   - fixated

Lexical Resource

Negative adjectives	Related Noun

48. Fierce   fight/argument
- violent
- ferocious
- brutal
- severe

49. Filthy   place/area/smell
- grimy
- muddy
- mucky
- grubby

50. Finicky   idea/decision/person
- fastidious
- fussy
- picky
- choosy

51. Flashy   show/idea/appearance
- ostentatious
- showy
- gaudy
- flamboyant

52. Flippant   remark/talk/idea/decision
- frivolous
- offhand
- dismissive
- superficial

53. Foolish   person/act/idea
- stupid
- silly
- idiotic
- unwise

54. Frantic   attitude/person
- worried
- frenzied
- frenetic
- hysterical

Negative adjectives	Related Nouns

55. Fretful person/behavior/act
- worried
- anxious
- fussy
- agitated

56. Frightened person/animal
- scared
- terrified
- alarmed
- startled

57. Furtive act/behavior/talk/nature
- secretive
- stealthy
- surreptitious
- sneaky

58. Greedy person/animal
- gluttonous
- voracious
- hungry
- ravenous

59. Grieving person/situation/time
- inconsolable
- anguished
- sorrowful
- brokenhearted

60. Grouchy person/being
- bad-tempered
- complaining
- grumpy
- crabby

61. Gruesome act/situation/story
- grisly
- ghastly
- horrible
- horrific

Lexical Resource

Negative adjectives	Related Nouns

62. Grumpy   person/being
- irritable
- cranky
- cantankerous
- cross

63. Guileful   plot/person/idea
- crafty
- dodgy (British)
- crafty
- devious

64. Gullible   person/child
- naive
- susceptible
- easy to fool
- innocent

65. Harmful   person/object/animal
- damaging
- injurious
- destructive
- detrimental

66. Heavy   rain/heart
- weighty
- profound
- weighty
- intense

67. Helpless   old man/patient/being
- powerless
- susceptible
- weak
- feeble

68. Hesitant   person/nature/decision
- uncertain
- cautious
- tentative
- diffident

Negative adjectives	Related Nouns

69. Homeless   person/poor/animal
- vagrant
- dispossessed
- destitute
- down-and-out

70. Horrible   act/movie/story/situation
- horrifying
- awful
- terrible
- nasty

71. Hungry (N)   person/animal/attitude
- starving
- famished
- ravenous
- greedy

72. Hurt   soul/feeling/person
- distress
- upset
- sorrowful
- sad

73. Ignorant   child/person
- unaware
- uninformed
- badly informed
- oblivious

74. Ill   person/animal
- unwell
- qualmish
- poorly
- sick

75. Irresolute   situation/decision/act
- indecisive
- vacillating
- unsure
- hesitant

Lexical Resource

Negative adjectives	Related Nouns

76. **Jealous**   person/nature
- envious
- desirous
- green-eyed
- covetous

77. **Jittery**   person/situation
- nervous
- nervy
- jumpy
- edgy

78. **Lacking**   item/thing/situation
- missing
- absent
- wanting
- deficient

79. **Lazy**   person/one/being
- indolent
- idle
- lethargic
- languid

80. **Lonely** (N)   place/heart/person
- forlorn
- lost
- lonesome
- alone

81. **Malicious**   jealousy/thought/person
- hateful
- spiteful
- malevolent
- mean

82. **Materialistic**   person/attitude
- money-oriented
- worldly
- selfish
- grasping

Negative adjectives	Related Nouns

83. **Mean**   nature/attitude/person
- selfish
- self-centered
- egoistic
- spiteful

84. **Mysterious (N)**   situation/place/time
- strange
- unexplained
- inexplicable
- unsolved

85. **Naïve**   person/one
- inexperienced
- immature
- adolescent
- raw

86. **Nasty**   person/behavior
- spiteful
- mean
- malicious
- vicious

87. **Naughty**   person/attitude
- disobedient
- bad
- badly behaved
- wicked

88. **Nervous**   person/being
- anxious
- worried
- edgy
- jumpy

89. **Noisy**   place/thing/situation
- loud
- deafening
- earsplitting
- deafening

Negative adjectives	Related Nouns
90. **Obnoxious**	person/situation
• loathsome	
• hateful	
• horrible	
• insufferable	
91. **Outrageous**	Person/act/behavior
• shameful	
• shocking	
• disgraceful	
• offensive	
92. **Panicky**	person/animal
• frightened	
• scared	
• alarmed	
• fearful	
93. **Pathetic**	situation/time/condition
• wretched	
• dismal	
• sad	
• pitiable	
94. **Possessive**	person/attitude
• jealous	
• domineering	
• controlling	
• scheming	
95. **Quarrelsome**	person/nature/attitude
• argumentative	
• cantankerous	
• difficult	
• irritable	
96. **Repulsive**	attitude/act/behavior
• disgusting	
• revolting	
• nauseating	
• hideous	

Negative adjectives	Related Nouns
97. **Ruthless**	person/nature/attitude
• cruel	
• callous	
• brutal	
• pitiless	
98. **Sad**	person/nature/attitude
• depressing	
• gloomy	
• cheerless	
• miserable	
99. **Scary**	person/nature/attitude
• frightening	
• creepy	
• chilling	
• terrifying	
100. **Secretive (N)**	situation/plot/person
• enigmatic	
• mysterious	
• reticent	
• reserved	
101. **Selfish**	person/attitude
• self-centered	
• egotistical	
• self-seeking	
• self-interested	
102. **Silly**	mistake/act/attitude
• stupid	
• ridiculous	
• impractical	
• childish	
103. **Slow**	act/behavior/decision
• sluggish	
• unhurried	
• measured	
• deliberate	

Lexical Resource

Negative adjectives	Related Nouns

104. Sneaky act/behavior/person
- devious
- sly
- shifty
- underhanded

105. Snobbish act/behavior/person
- supercilious
- stuck-up
- arrogant
- snooty

106. Sore result/situation/act
- painful
- stinging
- uncomfortable
- aching

107. Spendthrift person/behavior/attitude
- wastrel
- squanderer
- compulsive shopper
- fritterer

108. Squeamish person/behavior/attitude
- easily upset
- prudish
- straitlaced
- fastidious

109. Stingy person/behavior/attitude
- miserly
- parsimonious
- sparing
- grudging

110. Strange person/behavior/attitude
- odd
- bizarre
- outlandish
- eccentric

Negative adjectives	Related Nouns
111. Sulky	person/behavior/attitude
• morose	
• cross	
• petulant	
• sullen	
112. Tacky	person/behavior/attitude
• cheap	
• nasty	
• low	
• tawdry	
113. Tense	person/attitude
• stressed	
• edgy	
• overwrought	
• apprehensive	
114. Terrible	place/location/attitude
• awful	
• dreadful	
• very bad	
• appalling	
115. Testy	person/attitude
• bad-tempered	
• irritable	
• grumpy	
• impatient	
116. Thick-skinned	person/attitude
• insensitive	
• obtuse	
• unconcerned	
• impervious	
117. Thoughtless	person/attitude
• inconsiderate	
• unkind	
• uncaring	
• insensitive	

Lexical Resource

Negative adjectives	Related Nouns

118. Threatening   person/attitude/behavior
- intimidating
- bullying
- menacing
- hostile

119. Tight   Situation/person/attitude
- taut
- stretched
- tense
- stiff

120. Timid   person/animal/nature
- nervous
- shy
- fearful
- timorous

121. Tired (N)   person/animal
- weary
- exhausted
- worn-out
- drained

122. Tiresome   work/situation/job
- annoying
- irritating
- tedious
- wearisome

123. Troubled   situation/person
- bothered
- disturbed
- uneasy
- distressed

124. Truculent   person/attitude/behavior
- hostile
- bad-tempered
- defiant
- argumentative

Negative adjectives	Related Nouns

125. Undesirable   work/person/assignment
- unwanted
- unwelcome
- uninvited
- objectionable

126. Unsuitable   work/person/assignment
- inappropriate
- not fitting
- unfitted
- incongruous

127. Unsure   work/situation/duty
- uncertain
- doubtful
- irresolute
- dubious

128. Upset   person/one
- aflutter
- disturbed
- unquiet
- dithery

129. Uptight   person/one
- tense
- anxious
- bothered
- edgy

130. Vague   idea/situation
- indistinct
- unclear
- indistinguishable
- hazy

131. Vengeful   person/one/act
- revengeful
- vindictive
- rancorous
- implacable

Negative adjectives	Related Nouns
132. Venomous	animal/weapon/attack

- poisonous
- deadly
- toxic
- lethal

| **133. Volatile** | situation/time/behavior |

- unstable
- unpredictable
- explosive
- hot-blooded

| **134. Voracious** | person/animal/attitude |

- insatiable
- hungry
- ravenous
- gluttonous

| **135. Vulgar** | comment/talk/behavior |

- rude
- offensive
- crude
- improper

| **136. Wary** | person/one/character |

- suspicious
- distrustful
- chary
- shy

| **137. Wasteful** | person/one/character |

- extravagant
- lavish
- uneconomical
- careless

| **138. Weak** | person/one/character |

- frail
- puny
- scrawny
- pathetic

Negative adjectives	Related Nouns

139. Weary   person/one/character
- tired out
- sleepy
- exhausted
- worn out

140. Wicked   person/one/character
- evil
- bad
- wrong
- depraved

141. Worried   Person/being/someone
- concerned
- anxious
- apprehensive
- nervous

142. Worthless   thing/person
- of no value
- insignificant
- valueless
- useless

143. Wretched   person/situation
- miserable
- desolate
- heartbroken
- pitiful

144. Expensive   thing/area
- luxurious
- classy
- posh
- exclusive

145. Zany   person/situation
- crazy
- madcap
- screwball
- wacky

A Story, the Teaser

Once, a miserable person, Zing, tried to come out of his pathetic life to find happiness, but he came across many more wretched moments. He tried to seek contentment but; everywhere, he experienced a vague and undesirable situation. He met a person and thought he was a nice man, as that man gave him some money to spend. But, to his surprise, that man was wacky. He was a crazy person. The currency was counterfeit.

After sometime, a tired saint approached Zing. The saint was exhausted and weary from a long walk. He begged Zing to support him with some money to survive. Zing thought that saint to be a miser and thrifty. He was wearing a gold chain around his wrinkled neck.

Having met the man who gave fake money and thrifty saint, Zing concluded that life is zany, desolate and inapt for him. He asked God to call him to heaven. God rejected his appeal.

God asked him to help that saint who was wearing a phony gold chain. Zing was supposed to find more miserable person than him. The god was testing his attitude.

Task : Find out all the adjectives you find in the above story.

Points to Ponder...

Almost all these adjectives can be converted into Abstract Nouns.

Say: Expensive.....Expensiveness

Tired.....Tiredness

True....Truth

Be prepared to convert adjectives into nouns by Nominalization in 'A Book of Lexical Resource' Part 2 (B2 CEFR).

Chapter 3: Adjective: Thematic Range/Variant categories

Adjectives of Appearance:

Looks or visage of any person/place/scene/picture/situation/location/thing can be qualified by following Positive and Negative adjectives.

1. Attractive
2. Average
3. Beautiful
4. Blue-eyed
5. Bloody
6. Blushing
7. Bright
8. Clean
9. Clear
10. Cloudy
11. Colorful
12. Crowded
13. Cute
14. Dark
15. Drab
16. Distinct
17. Dull
18. Elegant
19. Excited
20. Fancy
21. Filthy
22. Glamorous
23. Gleaming
24. Gorgeous
25. Graceful
26. Grotesque
27. Handsome
28. Homely
29. Light
30. Long
31. Magnificent
32. Misty
33. Motionless
34. Muddy
35. Old-fashioned
36. Plain
37. Poised
38. Precious
39. Quaint
40. Shiny
41. Smoggy
42. Sparkling
43. Spotless
44. Stormy
45. Strange
46. Ugly
47. Ugliest
48. Unsightly
49. Unusual
50. Wide-eyed

- It looks **fancy.** What an **ugly** thing!
- She is **glamorous.**
- The sky is **cloudy.** It is a **stormy** situation, today.

Adjectives of Condition/Situation:

State or form of any person/place/scene/picture/situation/location/ thing can be qualified by following Positive and Negative adjectives.

1. Active
2. Alive
3. Annoying
4. Appalling
5. Awful
6. Bad
7. Beautiful
8. Better
9. Breakable
10. Busy
11. Clumsy
12. Dead
13. Different
14. Difficult
15. Doubtful
16. Drastic
17. Dreadful
18. Easy
19. Enhanced
20. Fragile
21. Frail
22. Ghastly
23. Gifted
24. Healthier
25. Helpful
26. Helpless
27. Horrible
28. Important
29. Impossible
30. Improved
31. Modern
32. Mushy
33. Odd
34. Open
35. Outstanding
36. Passive
37. Poor
38. Powerful
39. Prickly
40. Puzzled
41. Real
42. Recovered
43. Rich
44. Shocking
45. Shy
46. Sleepy
47. Super
48. Superior
49. Talented
50. Tame
51. Tender
52. Terrible
53. Tough
54. Wandering
55. Weird
56. Wrong

- This **city** is **alive.**
- This is a **shocking situation.**
- Don't go away from an **important state of affairs.**
- **Modern things** are liked by all.
- These are the **recovered items** from the thief.

Adjectives of Feelings/Situation: (Bad)

Human beings and animals have feelings and emotions. Following negative adjectives express the approach or behavior of a being.

1. Abhorrent
2. Aggravated
3. Agitated
4. Angry
5. Annoyed
6. Anxious
7. Appalling
8. Apprehensive
9. Ashamed
10. Awful
11. Bad
12. Bemused
13. Bewildered
14. Black
15. Blue
16. Bored
17. Bothered
18. Bruised
19. Clumsy
20. Combative
21. Condemned
22. Confused
23. Cranky
24. Crazy
25. Creepy
26. Defeated
27. Defiant
28. Depressed
29. Detestable
30. Discomfited
31. Disconcerted
32. Disgusted
33. Disgusting
34. Dispossessed
35. Distasteful
36. Disturbed
37. Disturbing
38. Dizzy
39. Down
40. Dreadful
41. Dull
42. Egotistical
43. Embarrassed
44. Envious
45. Errant
46. Famished
47. Fanatical
48. Fated
49. Fearful
50. Feeble
51. Fierce
52. Foolish
53. Forlorn
54. Frantic
55. Frightened
56. Green-eyed
57. Grieving
58. Grumpy
59. Haughty
60. Helpless

61. Homeless
62. Humiliated
63. Hungry
64. Hurt
65. Ill
66. Inconsolable
67. Inexplicable
68. Itchy
69. Jealous
70. Jittery
71. Languid
72. Lazy
73. Livid
74. Loathsome
75. Lonely
76. Maladroit
77. Malevolent
78. Malicious
79. Mortified
80. Mysterious
81. Mystified
82. Nasty
83. Naughty
84. Nauseating
85. Nervous
86. Nutty
87. Objectionable
88. Obnoxious
89. Outrageous
90. Panicky
91. Perturbed
92. Poorly
93. Prickly
94. Ravenous
95. Repugnant
96. Repulsive
97. Revolting
98. Scary
99. Selfish
100. Shamed
101. Sore
102. Starved
103. Starving
104. Tense
105. Terrible
106. Testy
107. Thoughtless
108. Tired
109. Troubled
110. Uncomfortable
111. Ungainly
112. Uninterested
113. Unsafe
114. Upset
115. Uptight
116. Wayward
117. Weary
118. Wicked
119. Worried
120. Zany

- I have a **bad** feeling.
- He feels **disgusted**
- Don't feel **annoyed.**
- This situation is **dreadful.**
- It seems **mystified.**

Adjectives of Feelings/Situations: (Good)

Italic words are adjectives for nouns.

- Please keep an *enthusiastic* **outlook**
- Our **approach** is *amazing.*
- Have a *fabulous* **manner**.
- Their **position** is *high and fair.*
- *Comforting* **thought** is *agreeable.*

1. Accommodating
2. Agreeable
3. Amazing
4. Amused
5. Amusing
6. Appealing
7. Auspicious
8. Benevolent
9. Booming
10. Bouncing
11. Brave
12. Calm
13. Charming
14. Cheerful
15. Chirpy
16. Comfortable
17. Comforted
18. Conquering
19. Contented
20. Cooperative
21. Courageous
22. Delightful
23. Determined
24. Divine
25. Eager

26. Ebullient
27. Effervescent
28. Elated
29. Enchanting
30. Encouraging
31. Energetic
32. Enjoyable
33. Enthralling
34. Enthusiastic
35. Excellent
36. Excited
37. Extraordinary
38. Exuberant
39. Fabulous
40. Fair
41. Fair-haired
42. Faithful
43. Fantastic
44. Fastidious
45. Festive
46. Fine
47. Friendly
48. Funny
49. Gentle
50. Glorious

Adjectives of Feelings/Situations (Good)

51. Good	80. Pleasing
52. Gratified	81. Pompous
53. Great	82. Proud
54. Happy	83. Relaxed
55. Healthy	84. Relieved
56. Heartening	85. Satisfying
57. Helpful	86. Side-splitting
58. Heroic	87. Silly
59. High-quality	88. Smiling
60. High-spirited	89. Solicitous
61. Hilarious	90. Spirited
62. In good spirits	91. Splendid
63. In the pink	92. Subservient
64. Jolly	93. Successful
65. Joyous	94. Sympathetic
66. Jubilant	95. Thankful
67. Kind	96. Thoughtful
68. Lively	97. Tranquil
69. Lovely	98. Unwavering
70. Lucky	99. Victorious
71. Magnificent	100. Vivacious
72. Merry	101. Welcoming
73. Nice	102. Wholehearted
74. Obedient	103. Willing
75. Obliging	104. Witty
76. Perfect	105. Wonderful
77. Placid	106. Zealous
78. Pleasant	
79. Pleased	

- A perfect man becomes victorious.
- Lucky is the one who is happy.
- My friend is nice and zealous.
- I have a lovely and joyous feelings.
- His placid nature is wonderful.

Adjectives of Shapes of things/places/person/ building:

1. Aerodynamic	31. Curly
2. Angular	32. Curved
3. Rounded	33. Curvilinear
4. Arched	34. Curvy
5. Asymmetrical	35. Cylindrical
6. Bent	36. Deformed
7. Bowed	37. Diamond
8. Bow-shaped	38. Disc-shaped
9. Branched	39. Dished
10. Bulbous	40. Domed
11. Chubby	41. Dome-shaped
12. Chunky	42. Fleshy
13. Circle	43. Forked
14. Closed	44. Furrowed
15. Coiled	45. Heart-shaped
16. Concave	46. Hexagonal
17. Concentric	47. Hollow
18. Congruent	48. Hunched
19. Conical	49. In a circle
20. Contorted	50. Jagged
21. Contoured	51. Kite-shaped
22. Convex	52. Notched
23. Convoluted	53. Oblong
24. Corpulent	54. Octagonal
25. Corrugated	55. Octahedral
26. Creased	56. Outsized
27. Crooked	57. Oval
28. Crystalline	58. Parallel
29. Cubical	59. Peewee
30. Cuboids	60. Pentagonal

Adjectives of Shapes of things/places/person/building

61. Perpendicular
62. Piercing
63. Pleated
64. Plumb
65. Pointed
66. Pointy
67. Pyramidal
68. Quadrilateral
69. Rangy
70. Rectangular
71. Reshaped
72. Ribbed
73. Rippled
74. Round
75. Ruffled
76. Saw-like
77. Scrawny
78. Semi circle
79. Serrated
80. Sharp
81. Spherical
82. Spiral
83. Square
84. Star-shaped
85. Steep
86. Stooped
87. Stout
88. Straight
89. Symmetrical
90. Tapered
91. Three Dimensional
92. Triangular
93. Tucked
94. Twisted
95. Two Dimensional
96. Undersized

Examples:

- **An arched passage** always welcomes me.
- **This zigzag road** goes to market.
- **These serrated teeth** are dangerous.
- Sugar is **crystalline shaped.**
- **A stooped man** is very old.
- A **semi circle** is always half of the **circle.**
- **Chubby** cheeks are pulled by all.
- I have an **oval** shaped dining table which has **twisted** legs of wood.

Adjectives of Size of
Building/Thing/Person/Animal/Space:

1.	Big	34.	Minor
2.	Bony	35.	Minuscule
3.	Bottomless	36.	Narrow
4.	Broad	37.	Obese
5.	Bulky	38.	Overweight
6.	Colossal	39.	Petite
7.	Corpulent	40.	Plane
8.	Deep	41.	Plump
9.	Diminutive	42.	Pocket-sized
10.	Dumpy	43.	Puny
11.	Elfin	44.	Scrawny
12.	Emaciated	45.	Shallow
13.	Enormous	46.	Short
14.	Epic	47.	Skeletal
15.	Fat	48.	Skinny
16.	Gargantuan	49.	Slender
17.	Giant	50.	Small
18.	Gigantic	51.	Soaring
19.	Grand	52.	Spacious
20.	Great	53.	Squat
21.	Heavy	54.	Stout
22.	Hefty	55.	Substantial
23.	High	56.	Tall
24.	Huge	57.	Teensy
25.	Immense	58.	Teeny
26.	Jumbo	59.	Teeny-Tiny
27.	Large	60.	Thin
28.	Lean	61.	Tiny
29.	Little	62.	Undersized
30.	Low	63.	Unfathomable
31.	Mammoth	64.	Vast
32.	Massive	65.	Whooping
33.	Miniature	66.	Wide

My Notes

Note:
Try to create a group of words with similar meaning as this one.
Mammoth / Enormous/ Huge /Massive/ Immense /Epic
Colossal / Gargantuan

Adjectives of Time:
Action/Person/World/Era/Age/Period
(Adv = Adverb   Pre. = Preposition)

1. Abrupt
2. Abundant
3. Accurate
4. Adult
5. Aged
6. Ago
7. Ahead (Adv.)
8. Ancient
9. Antiquated
10. Antique
11. Archaic
12. Bad
13. Behind (Adv.)
14. Breathtaking
15. Brief
16. Brisk
17. Childish
18. Closing
19. Contemporary
20. Creative
21. Current
22. Deceased
23. Delayed
24. Early (Adv.)
25. Enough
26. Epic
27. Epigrammatic
28. Existing
29. Extended
30. Extensive
31. Fabulous
32. Fast (Adv)
33. Fleeing
34. Flourishing
35. Future
36. Good
37. Grown-up
38. Hasty
39. Hurried
40. Immediate
41. Infant
42. Last (Adv.)
43. Late (Adv.)
44. Latest
45. Limited
46. Little
47. Local
48. Long (Adv.)
49. Long-ago
50. Modern
51. Modern-day
52. More (Adv.)
53. Much (Adv.)
54. Nippy
55. Old
56. Old-Fashioned
57. On hand
58. On the dot
59. Opening
60. Out-dated
61. Past (Pre)
62. Pending
63. Plenty of
64. Postponed

Adjectives of Time: Action/Person/World/Era/Age/Period

65.	Preceding	83.	Short
66.	Prehistoric	84.	Short-lived
67.	Premature	85.	Slow
68.	Present	86.	Sluggish
69.	Previous	87.	Speedy
70.	Primal	88.	Splendid
71.	Primitive	89.	Squat
72.	Primordial	90.	Succinct
73.	Prompt	91.	Sudden
74.	Prompt	92.	Swift
75.	Prosperous	93.	Traditional
76.	Punctual	94.	Unhurried
77.	Quick	95.	Upcoming
78.	Rapid	96.	Veteran
79.	Ripened	97.	Weathered
80.	Scanty	98.	Wonderful
81.	Scarce	99.	Young
82.	Seasoned	100.	Youthful

Some Examples:

1.   In this modern era, we have become technocrats.
2.   We can't catch fleeing time.
3.   A little time is left to save the natural resources.
4.   Antique things are worthy.
5.   A succinct episode is always inspiring.

A note: Readers should use these adjectives with related nouns so that Collocation is justified. Rather than memorizing these words, seeking advice from your mentor is must.
By process of Nominalization adverbs are usually formed by adding -ly after an adjective.
• Slow.....Slowly
• Prompt.....Promptly
• Brief..... Briefly
• Quick..... Quickly (but not....fast to fastly...it is fast to fast..)

Adjectives of Taste/Touch/ Look/ Texture/Surface:

Many items such as food, liquids, crystals, vapor, fumes, smoke, and other things are defined by these adjectives.

1.	Acidic	31.	Dusty
2.	Appetizing	32.	Edible
3.	Aromatic	33.	Fatty
4.	Artificial	34.	Filthy
5.	Bitter	35.	Flaky
6.	Blended	36.	Flavorful
7.	Blistering	37.	Fluffy
8.	Boiling	38.	Foamy
9.	Brackish	39.	Freezing
10.	Brawny	40.	Fried
11.	Breezy	41.	Frothy
12.	Broken	42.	Frozen
13.	Bubbly	43.	Fusty
14.	Bumpy	44.	Fuzzy
15.	Chilly	45.	Glittering
16.	Cold	46.	Glossy
17.	Coloured	47.	Glutinous
18.	Cool	48.	Gooey
19.	Creamy	49.	Greasy
20.	Creepy	50.	Grubby
21.	Crooked	51.	Gummy
22.	Cuddly	52.	Hard
23.	Curly	53.	Hot
24.	Damaged	54.	Icy
25.	Damp	55.	Insipid
26.	Decayed	56.	Invigorating
27.	Delectable	57.	Juicy
28.	Delicious	58.	Loose
29.	Dirty	59.	Luscious
30.	Dry	60.	Melted

Adjectives of Taste/Touch/Look/Texture/Surface

61. Mouth watering
62. Muddy
63. Nebulous
64. Non-organic
65. Nourishing
66. Nutritious
67. Oily
68. Opaque
69. Organic
70. Palatable
71. Peppery
72. Perfumed
73. Piquant
74. Plastic
75. Prickly
76. Pungent
77. Rainy
78. Razor-sharp
79. Ripe
80. Roasted
81. Roasting
82. Rotten
83. Rough
84. Saline
85. Salty
86. Savory
87. Scattered
88. Scented
89. Scrumptious
90. Searing
91. Seasoned
92. Shaggy
93. Shaky
94. Sharp
95. Shining
96. Shivering
97. Silky
98. Sizzling
99. Sleek
100. Slimy
101. Slippery
102. Smeared
103. Smooth
104. Soft
105. Soiled
106. Solid
107. Soothe
108. Sour
109. Spicy
110. Squashy
111. Stale
112. Steady
113. Sticky
114. Stimulating
115. Strong
116. Succulent
117. Sugary
118. Sultry
119. Sweet
120. Synthetic
121. Tangy
122. Tarnished

123. Tart
124. Tasteless
125. Tasty
126. Tender
127. Tight
128. Transparent
129. Uneven
130. Viscous
131. Warm
132. Weak
133. Wet
134. Wooden
135. Yummy
136. Zesty

Some examples:

1. Some food items are **very spicy.**
2. This sweet dish is **yummy.**
3. **Stale food** should not be consumed.
4. We avoid consuming **oily food**.
5. **Sugary** food is liked by children.
6. The surface of this table is **uneven but smooth.**
7. We may slip on **slippery surfaces**.
8. The **bumpy roads** make me sick.
9. This **shining surface** is liked by all.
10. I walked on the **rough road.**

An assignment:

Choose the best qualitative words (adjectives) for Pizza, Tomato Soup, Burger, Cake, Butter and Cheese. Can you pick out all the adjectives of food items that you eat or like? When you do this, make a paragraph about food dishes that you like the most.

Chapter 4. Determiners

Now let us be sure to use at least one of these words to quantify any noun, singular or plural, which is used in a sentence. Almost all determiners are classified among Adjectives.

Determiners: Quantity/Volume/Amount/Number/Weight/Portion

1. A few
2. A bit of
3. A great deal of
4. A large number of
5. A little
6. A lot of
7. A pinch of
8. A quantity of
9. A small number of
10. A vast number of
11. Abundant
12. Additional
13. Adequate
14. All
15. Ample of
16. Any
17. As much as
18. Blank
19. Bountiful
20. Copious
21. Countable
22. Countless
23. Each
24. Either
25. Empty
26. Enough
27. Every
28. Excess
29. Extra
30. Fathomable
31. Few
32. Generous
33. Handful
34. Hardly any
35. Heavy
36. Hefty
37. Immeasurable
38. Incalculable
39. Inestimable
40. Infinite
41. Innumerable
42. Large amount of
43. Left over
44. Light
45. Loads of
46. Lots of
47. Many
48. Mouthful
49. Much
50. Neither
51. Numerous
52. Overabundance
53. Plenty
54. Plentiful
55. Plethora of
56. Profound
57. Profuse
58. Robust

59. Scanty
60. Several
61. Sizeable
62. Some
63. Spare
64. Surplus
65. Substantial
66. Sufficient
67. Superfluity

68. Superfluous
69. Tremendous
70. Uncountable
71. Unfathomable
72. Unstated
73. Various
74. Vast amount of
75. Very less
76. Weighty

Examples:
- There is **hardly** any water in this tank to use.
- **Various** English books are written by S. Raja.
- We need **substantial** amount of food to survive.
- The earth has **unstated** amount of natural resources.
- There is **plethora of** arguments from the opposition.

Remember, these quantifiers are for both countable, and uncountable types of nouns. Try to imagine the thing/ people/ any object/ place after it and write in the notebook. Speak aloud to practice.

The detailed understanding of countable and uncountable nouns is in the book 'The Grammar Made Easy' by S. Raja.

A Note from the writer:
Dear reader,
The detailed understanding of Adjectives, its degrees, Royal Order of Adjective is well explained in the forthcoming book, *'The Grammar made Easy'* by S. Raja

Traits:
The qualities of Human beings/Animals

We know so many nearest or dearest people in the world. We need to explain their characters/attitude/nature/behavior and other qualities as well.
We can split these Traits into three categories:
Positive, Negative and Neutral

We shall now read and add new words to our vocabulary. Remember we haven't placed all the words here.

Now let's begin with positive qualities. Try to find as many as people you know and remember them by matching these qualities. It's a fun and activity both.

Positive:
Traits/personality/character/qualities

	Quality	Possible Synonyms and Nearest Words
1.	Accessible	reachable/understandable/omnipresent
2.	Active	productive/dynamic/busy
3.	Adaptable	all-round/versatile/protean
4.	Admirable	commendable/worthy/laudable
5.	Adorable	darling/dear/winning
6.	Adventurous	daring/audacious/venturous
7.	Aggressive	ambitious/enterprising/assertive
8.	Agreeable	gratifying/nice/good
9.	Alert	attentive/observant/watchful
10.	Ambitious	determined/striving/motivated
11.	Amiable	friendly/sociable/affable
12.	Anticipated	eager/open-eyed/watchful
13.	Appreciative	grateful/admiring/eulogistic
14.	Articulate	eloquent/coherent/clear
15.	Ascetic	austere/monastic/Spartan

Positive Qualities
Traits/personality/character/qualities

	Quality	Possible Synonyms and Nearest Words
16.	Aspiring	hopeful/aspirant/ambitious
17.	Athletic	sporty/agile/nimble
18.	Attractive	good-looking/striking/eye-catching
19.	Available	reachable/free/omnipresent
20.	Balanced	clear-headed/fair/impartial
21.	Benevolent	good-hearted/humane/benign
22.	Brainy	intelligent/bright/ intellectual
23.	Breezy	cheerful/jolly/jovial
24.	Brilliant	dazzling/alluring/bright
25.	Calm	serene/peaceful/cool
26.	Capable	competent/able/skilled
27.	Captivating	charming/alluring/enchanting
28.	Careful	cautious/vigilant/watchful
29.	Caring	kind/thoughtful/considerate
30.	Cautious	alert/vigilant/watchful
31.	Cerebral	brainy/logical/high-brow
32.	Challenging	arduous/demanding/hellacious
33.	Charismatic	magnetic/alluring/compelling
34.	Charming	amiable/appealing/luring
35.	Cheerful	jovial/happy/blithesome
36.	Chummy	friendly/sociable/buddy-buddy
37.	Circumspect	prudent/cautious/guarded
38.	Clean	untarnished/spotless/fair
39.	Clear-headed	sane/lucid/balanced
40.	Clever	brainy/ingenious/savvy
41.	Colorful	brilliant/gay/vibrant
42.	Compassionate	sympathetic/concerned/kind
43.	Conciliatory	appeasing/pacifying/ peace-making
44.	Confident	convinced/self-assured/positive
45.	Conscientious	reliable/careful/meticulous
46.	Considerate	caring/thoughtful/understanding
47.	Constant	unvarying/steady/regular

Positive Qualities
Traits/personality/character/qualities

Quality	Possible Synonyms and Nearest Words
48. Contemplative	pensive/melancholy/thoughtful
49. Cooperative	helpful/supportive/accommodating
50. Courageous	brave/gutsy/audacious
51. Courteous	polite/well-mannered/chivalrous
52. Creative	imaginative/artistic/ingenious
53. Cultured	educated/sophisticated/civilized
54. Daring	audacious/courageous/intrepid
55. Debonair	suave/elegant/well-groomed
56. Decent	polite/respectable/civilized
57. Decisive	key/influential/significant
58. Dedicated	devoted/committed/keen
59. Dignified	distinguished/decorous/noble
60. Directed	determined/aimed/intended
61. Disciplined	self-controlled/temperate/resolved
62. Discreet	tactful/cautious/diplomatic
63. Dutiful	obedient/submissive/compliant
64. Dynamic	lively/active/vibrant
65. Earnest	serious/grave/sober
66. Ebullient	jovial/happy/jaunty
67. Educated	cultured/skilled/erudite
68. Efficient	capable/well-organized/efficacious
69. Elegant	graceful/decent/chic
70. Eloquent	expressive/fluent/articulate
71. Empathetic	sympathetic/concerned/kind
72. Energetic	brisk/lively/bouncy
73. Enthusiastic	passionate/ardent/fervent
74. Esthetic	handsome/good-looking/engaging
75. Exciting	electrifying/stimulating/exhilarating
76. Extraordinary	bizarre/peculiar/amazing
77. Fair	just/reasonable/handsome
78. Faithful	authentic/truthful/honest
79. Famous	well-known/eminent/popular

Positive Qualities
Traits/personality/character/qualities

Quality	Possible Synonyms and Nearest Words
80. Farsighted	intuitive/telepathic/perceptive
81. Falsified	blissful/joyous/glad
82. Firm	determined/confident/sanguine
83. Flexible	reasonable/adaptable/easygoing
84. Focused	attentive/engrossed/rapt
85. Forgiving	merciful/lenient/magnanimous
86. Forthright	straightforward/frank/candid
87. Freethinking	progressive/liberal/enlightened
88. Friendly	gracious/welcoming/affable
89. Fun loving	joyful/high spirited/light-hearted
90. Gallant	brave/courageous/valiant
91. Generous	open-handed/kind/munificent
92. Gentle	mild/calm/tender
93. Genuine	real/undisputed/authentic
94. Glamorous	alluring/enchanting/stunning
95. Good-natured	pleasant/friendly/cheerful
96. Gracious	courteous/polite/well-mannered
97. Guileless	frank/candid/straightforward
98. Hardworking	meticulous/painstaking/assiduous
99. Healthy	fit/hale and hearty/well
100. Hearty	energetic/jovial/cheerful
101. Helpful	obliging/cooperative/supportive
102. Heroic	daring/valiant/gallant
103. High-minded	moralizing/didactic/straitlaced
104. High-spirited	lively/exuberant/vivacious
105. Honest	sincere/frank/candid
106. Honorable	admirable/praise-worthy/respectable
107. Humble	modest/meek/self-effacing
108. Humorous	amusing/hilarious/entertaining
109. Idealistic	hopeful/optimistic/zealous
110. Imaginative	inventive/ingenious/creative
111. Impressive	striking/notable/inspiring
112. Incisive	keen/perceptive/insightful
113. Incorruptible	principled/honest/morally upright

Positive Qualities
Traits/ personality/ character/ qualities

Quality	Possible Synonyms and Nearest Words
114. Individualistic	unique/peculiar/exceptional
115. Innocent	blameless/clean/childlike
116. Innovative	creative/novel/pioneering
117. Inoffensive	harmless/mild/benign
118. Inquisitive	curious/questioning/inquiring
119. Insightful	perceptive/thoughtful/prudent
120. Insouciant	debonair/light hearted/blithe
121. Intellectual	thinker/brainy/dexterous
122. Intelligent	clever/sharp/bright
123. Intuitive	perceptive/innate/instinctive
124. Invulnerable	invincible/unbeatable/indomitable
125. Kind	generous/munificent/giving
126. Knowledgeable	erudite/cognizant/mindful
127. Leisurely	unhurried/easy going/restful
128. Liberal	open-minded/tolerant/moderate
129. Lively	energetic/vigorous/vivacious
130. Logical	rational/reasonable/coherent
131. Lovable	endearing/adorable/congenial
132. Loyal	trustworthy/faithful/steadfast
133. Lyrical	emotional/poetic/romantic
134. Magnanimous	generous/noble/chivalrous
135. Many-sided	versatile/multitalented/all-rounder
136. Masculine	mannish/manly/virile
137. Mature	qualified/experienced/competent
138. Mellow	placid/calm/docile
139. Methodical	systematic/orderly/meticulous
140. Meticulous	careful/scrupulous/painstaking
141. Moderate	modest/reasonable/judicious
142. Modest	humble/demure/down to earth
143. Neat	orderly/efficient/careful
144. Obedient	dutiful/submissive/subservient
145. Objective	candid/fair/impartial
146. Observant	sharp-eyes/alert/attentive
147. Open	frank/open-hearted/guileless

Positive Qualities
Traits/personality/character/qualities

Quality	Possible Synonyms and Nearest Words
148. Optimistic	sanguine/buoyant/inspiring
149. Orderly	well-groomed/streamlined/logical
150. Organized	neat/regular/methodical
151. Passionate	fervent/ardent/zealous
152. Patient	enduring/tolerant/broad-minded
153. Patriotic	loyal/nationalist/jingoistic
154. Peaceful	non-violent/diplomatic/subtle
155. Perceptive	sensitive/insightful/observant
156. Perfectionist	obsessive/purist/stickler
157. Personable	friendly/affable/amiable
158. Persuasive	convincing/swaying/credible
159. Placid	cool/composed/docile
160. Playful	good-humored-natured/teasing
161. Polished	elegant/refined/sophisticated
162. Popular	admired/well-liked/accepted
163. Practical	sensible/realistic/reasonable
164. Precise	perfect/strict/particular
165. Principled	righteous/ethical/just
166. Profound	thoughtful/philosophical/insightful
167. Progressive	advanced/developed/civilized
168. Protean	expert/adjustable/flexible
169. Protective	caring/defensive/shielding
170. Providential	fortunate/lucky/fluky
171. Prudent	careful/cautious/discreet
172. Punctual	prompt/on the dot/apt
173. Pure	clean/untarnished/faultless
174. Purposeful	determined/focused/resolute
175. Quiet	calm/silent/hushed
176. Rational	reasonable/balanced/cogent
177. Realistic	sensible/practical/pragmatic
178. Reflective	thoughtful/philosophical/deep
179. Relaxed	stress-free/calm/tranquil
180. Reliable	dependable/steadfast/trustworthy

Positive Qualities
Traits/personality/character/qualities

	Quality	Possible Synonyms and Nearest Words
181.	Religious	pious/dutiful/spiritual
182.	Resourceful	inventive/ingenious/imaginative
183.	Respectful	polite/courteous/civil
184.	Responsible	accountable/in charge/liable
185.	Responsive	receptive/approachable/alert
186.	Reverential	respectful/reverent/polite
187.	Romantic	idealistic/passionate/loving
188.	Sage	wise/sagacious/erudite
189.	Sane	rational/reasonable/sensible
190.	Scholarly	learned/cerebral/intellectual
191.	Self-critical	ego less/humble/modest
192.	Selfless	unselfish/altruistic/humane
193.	Self-reliant	self-dependent/autonomous/independent
194.	Sensitive	responsive/aware/receptive
195.	Sentimental	emotional/poignant/nostalgic
196.	Seraphic	blissful/rapturous/ascetic
197.	Serious	sober/grave/somber
198.	Shrewd	sharp/smart/insightful
199.	Simple	straightforward/trouble-less/easy
200.	Skillful	dexterous/adroit/adept
201.	Sober	abstemious/temperate/moderate
202.	Sociable	friendly/genial/convivial
203.	Solid	firm/dependable/calculable
204.	Sophisticated	stylish/classic/chic
205.	Spontaneous	impulsive/fast/natural
206.	Sporting	fair/generous/relaxed
207.	Stable	firm/steady/established
208.	Steadfast	unwavering/resolute/dedicated
209.	Steady	firm/unmoved/balanced
210.	Stoic	patient/tolerant/fore-bearing
211.	Strong	brawny/well-built/burly
212.	Studious	bookish/scholarly/diligent
213.	Suave	polished/polite/debonair

Positive Qualities
Traits/personality/character/qualities

	Quality	Possible Synonyms and Nearest Words
214.	Subtle	delicate/clever/fine
215.	Sweet	cute/ charming/engaging
216.	Sympathetic	kind/compassionate/sensitive
217.	Systematic	methodical/regular/orderly
218.	Tasteful	sophisticated/refined/elegant
219.	Thorough	careful/systematic/meticulous
220.	Tidy	neat/organized/spick and span
221.	Tolerant	broad-minded/liberal/permissive
222.	Tractable	obedient/dutiful/polite
223.	Uncomplaining	accepting/patient/forgiving
224.	Understanding	thoughtful/considerate/selfless
225.	Upright	decent/honest/civilized
226.	Urbane	sophisticated/suave/cultured
227.	Venturesome	adventurous/enterprising/daring
228.	Vivacious	full of life/energetic/spirited
229.	Warm	affectionate/friendly/kind
230.	Well-bred	polite/mannerly/courteous
231.	Well-read	knowledgeable/educated/erudite
232.	Well-rounded	pleasing/all-round/well-formed
233.	Winning	charming/captivating/endearing
234.	Wise	prudent/sensible/judicious
235.	Witty	amusing/sharp/clever
236.	Youthful	young at heart/childlike/young
237.	Zealous	fervent/enthusiastic/keen
238.	Zestful	passionate/dynamic/energetic
239.	Zesty	invigorating/stimulating/bracing

Negative Qualities
Traits/personality/character/qualities
(Supported with some synonyms)
A few words have (N) means these words are of Neutral Quality as well.

1. **Abrasive**
   - rough
   - harsh
   - rude
2. **Abrupt**
   - rapid
   - hasty
   - rushed
3. **Aggressive**
   - violent
   - hostile
   - belligerent
4. **Agonizing**
   - excruciating
   - distressing
   - worrying
5. **Aimless**
   - worthless
   - purposeless
   - direction less
6. **Aloof**
   - distant
   - detached
   - unfriendly
7. **Amoral**
   - unprincipled
   - dishonorable
   - unscrupulous
8. **Angry**
   - annoyed
   - fuming
   - livid

9. **Antisocial**
   - disruptive
   - rebellious
   - inconsiderate
10. **Anxious (N)**
    - nervous
    - worried
    - concerned
11. **Apathetic**
    - indifferent
    - uninterested
    - droopy
12. **Arbitrary**
    - uninformed
    - illogical
    - capricious
13. **Argumentative**
    - quarrelsome
    - confrontational
    - awkward
14. **Arrogant**
    - conceited
    - egotistical
    - haughty
15. **Bizarre**
    - uncanny
    - wacky
    - strange
16. **Bland**
    - insipid
    - weak
    - featureless

Negative Qualities
Traits/personality/character/qualities
(Supported with some synonyms)

17. **Boisterous**
- unruly
- rowdy
- disorderly

18. **Brutal**
- atrocious
- vicious
- wicked

19. **Calculating**
- manipulative
- cunning
- devious

20. **Callous**
- heartless
- coldhearted
- uncaring

21. **Cantankerous**
- bad tempered
- irritable
- crabby

22. **Careless**
- lackadaisical
- slipshod
- hasty

23. **Clumsy**
- awkward
- inept
- gauche

24. **Coarse**
- uncouth
- vulgar
- foul-mouthed

25. **Cold**
- heart-less
- un-friendly
- gelid

26. **Colorless**
- dull
- drab
- uninteresting

27. **Complaining**
- tetchy
- crabby
- belligerent

28. **Compulsive**
- uncontrollable
- neurotic
- obsessive

29. **Conceited**
- proud
- smug
- snobbish

30. **Condemnatory**
- disapproving
- disparaging
- denouncing

31. **Contemptible**
- disgraceful
- shameful
- despicable

32. **Cowardly**
- gutless
- spineless
- craven

Negative Qualities
Traits/ personality/ character/ qualities
(Supported with some synonyms)

33. **Crass**
- insensitive
- tactless
- stupid

34. **Crazy**
- foolish
- unwise
- idiotic

35. **Criminal**
- unlawful
- illicit
- scandalous

36. **Crude**
- unsophisticated
- rough and ready
- unfinished

37. **Cruel**
- unkind
- vindictive
- pitiless

38. **Cynical**
- pessimistic
- skeptical
- suspicious

39. **Decadent**
- corrupt
- debauched
- depraved

40. **Deceitful**
- dishonest
- fraudulent
- devious

41. **Deceptive**
- misleading
- unreliable
- illusory

42. **Derogatory**
- deprecating
- offensive
- insulting

43. **Destructive**
- unhelpful
- harsh
- caustic

44. **Devious**
- deceitful
- scheming
- designing

45. **Disconcerting**
- distressing
- bewildering
- perplexing

46. **Discontented**
- dissatisfied
- unhappy
- malcontent

47. **Discouraging**
- hopeless
- gloomy
- daunting

48. **Discourteous**
- rude
- ill-mannered
- impolite

Negative Qualities
Traits/personality/character/qualities
(Supported with some synonyms)

49. **Dishonest**
- deceitful
- insincere
- fraudulent

50. **Disloyal**
- unfaithful
- treacherous
- fickle

51. **Disobedient**
- noncompliant
- insubordinate
- defiant

52. **Disorderly**
- unruly
- riotous
- antisocial

53. **Disorganized**
- muddled
- messy
- incompetent

54. **Disrespectful**
- impolite
- bad-mannered
- insolent

55. **Disruptive**
- troublesome
- unruly
- trouble making

56. **Dissonant**
- harsh
- jarring
- inharmonious

57. **Disturbing**
- worrying
- disquieting
- upsetting

58. **Dogmatic**
- rigid
- unbending
- inflexible

59. **Domineering**
- dictatorial
- dominant
- bossy

60. **Egocentric**
- inconsiderate
- selfish
- egotistic

61. **Envious**
- jealous
- green
- spiteful

62. **Erratic**
- irregular
- unreliable
- unpredictable

63. **Extravagant**
- profligate
- wasteful
- spendthrift

64. **Extremist**
- radical
- fanatic
- terrorist

Negative Qualities
Traits/personality/character/qualities
(Supported with some synonyms)

65. **Faithless**
- disloyal
- untrustworthy
- fickle

66. **False**
- phony
- fake
- bogus

67. **Fearful**
- frightened
- afraid
- timid

68. **Fickle**
- vacillating
- capricious
- indecisive

69. **Fiery (very angry)**
- blistering
- burning
- smoldering

70. **Flamboyant**
- showy
- gaudy
- lurid

71. **Foolish**
- imprudent
- reckless
- idiotic

72. **Forgetful**
- neglectful
- absentminded
- scatterbrained

73. **Fraudulent**
- deceitful
- deceptive
- sham

74. **Frightening**
- scary
- terrifying
- fearsome

75. **Gloomy**
- depressing
- dismal
- murky

76. **Graceless**
- clumsy
- ungainly
- gawky

77. **Greedy**
- gluttonous
- insatiable
- ravenous

78. **Grim**
- depressing
- dismal
- forbidding

79. **Gullible**
- naive
- susceptible
- easy to fool

80. **Hateful**
- horrible
- vile
- odious

Negative Qualities
Traits/personality/character/qualities
(Supported with some synonyms)

81. **Haughty**
    - proud
    - arrogant
    - snooty
82. **Hedonistic**
    - self-indulgent
    - riotous
    - wild
83. **Hesitant**
    - shy
    - doubtful
    - undecided
84. **Hidebound**
    - narrow-minded
    - prejudiced
    - conservative
85. **High-handed**
    - bossy
    - autocratic
    - imperious
86. **Hostile**
    - antagonistic
    - aggressive
    - unfriendly
87. **Ignorant**
    - unaware
    - bad-mannered
    - impolite
88. **Ill-mannered**
    - impolite
    - inappropriate
    - rude

89. **Imitative**
    - uninspired
    - hackneyed
    - trite
90. **Impatient**
    - annoyed
    - irritated
    - edgy
91. **Impractical**
    - pointless
    - unreasonable
    - unrealistic
92. **Imprudent**
    - reckless
    - irresponsible
    - hasty
93. **Impulsive**
    - impetuous
    - hurried
    - rash
94. **Inconsiderate**
    - selfish
    - thoughtless
    - insensitive
95. **Indecisive**
    - irresolute
    - hesitant
    - uncertain
96. **Inert**
    - sluggish
    - inactive
    - dormant

Negative Qualities
Traits/personality/character/qualities
(Supported with some synonyms)

97. **Inhibited**
- introverted
- repressed
- subdued

98. **Insecure**
- timid
- apprehensive
- self-doubting

99. **Insensitive**
- numb
- unfeeling
- insensate

100. **Insincere**
- dishonest
- two-faced
- disingenuous

101. **Insulting**
- abusive
- offensive
- insolent

102. **Intolerant**
- bigoted
- prejudiced
- narrow-minded

103. **Irascible**
- grumpy
- snappish
- touchy

104. **Irrational**
- foolish
- silly
- unreasonable

105. **Irreligious**
- profane
- ungodly
- unspiritual

106. **Irresponsible**
- reckless
- careless
- negligent

107. **Irreverent**
- disrespectful
- impertinent
- impudent

108. **Irritable**
- bad-tempered
- touchy
- tetchy

109. **Lazy**
- indolent
- sluggish
- languid

110. **Malicious**
- spiteful
- hateful
- malevolent

111. **Mechanical**
- emotionless
- involuntary
- unthinking

112. **Meddlesome**
- interfering
- intrusive
- nosy

Negative Qualities
Traits/personality/character/qualities
(Supported with some synonyms)

113. **Melancholic**
- miserable
- despondent
- sad

114. **Messy**
- chaotic
- muddled
- confused

115. **Miserable**
- down
- fed-up
- depressed

116. **Miserly**
- stingy
- penny-pinching
- tightfisted

117. **Misguided**
- erroneous
- imprudent
- foolish

118. **Mistaken**
- erroneous
- wrong
- incorrect

119. **Moody (N)**
- temperamental
- grumpy
- glum

120. **Morbid**
- sinister
- gruesome
- gloomy

121. **Naïve**
- inexperienced
- immature
- raw

122. **Narcissistic**
- egotistic
- selfish
- conceited

123. **Narrow-minded**
- prejudiced
- biased
- intolerant

124. **Negative**
- pessimistic
- non-constructive
- depressing

125. **Neglectful**
- careless
- slipshod
- remiss

126. **Neurotic**
- fearful
- phobic
- disturbed

127. **Nihilistic**
- hopeless
- cynical
- fatalistic

128. **Obnoxious**
- loathsome
- horrible
- detestable

Negative Qualities
Traits/personality/character/qualities
(Supported with some synonyms)

129. **Obsessive**
- fixated
- compulsive
- infatuated

130. **Odd**
- weird
- anomalous
- strange

131. **Offhand**
- discourteous
- inattentive
- brusque

132. **One-dimensional**
- crude
- naive
- unsophisticated

133. **One-sided**
- unfair
- biased
- misleading

134. **Opinionated**
- narrow-minded
- prejudiced
- dogmatic

135. **Opportunistic**
- pushy
- self-assertive
- competitive

136. **Oppressed**
- browbeaten
- subjugated
- broken

137. **Outrageous**
- disgraceful
- shameful
- shocking

138. **Paranoid**
- unreasonable
- mistrustful
- suspicious

139. **Passive**
- unreceptive
- inert
- inactive

140. **Pedantic**
- dull
- plodding
- arcane

141. **Perverse**
- wicked
- vicious
- obstinate

142. **Petty**
- less important
- minor
- trivial

143. **Plodding**
- slow
- poky
- lazy

144. **Pompous (N)**
- self-important
- arrogant
- pretentious

Negative Qualities
Traits/ personality/ character/ qualities
(Supported with some synonyms)

145. **Possessive**
- jealous
- domineering
- selfish

146. **Predatory**
- greedy
- rapacious
- voracious

147. **Prejudiced**
- biased
- intolerant
- bigoted

148. **Presumptuous**
- audacious
- arrogant
- conceited

149. **Pretentious**
- pompous
- showy
- ostentatious

150. **Prim**
- prudish
- stuffy
- pedantic

151. **Procrastinating**
- lethargic
- sluggish
- indolent

152. **Provocative**
- offensive
- insulting
- aggressive

153. **Reactionary (N)**
- intransigent
- diehard
- backward-looking

154. **Reactive**
- hasty
- unthinking
- immediate

155. **Regimental (N)**
- proud
- commanding
- dictating

156. **Regretful**
- apologetic
- repentant
- remorseful

157. **Repentant**
- sorry
- contrite
- penitent

158. **Repressed (N)**
- reserved
- self-conscious
- subdued

159. **Resentful**
- angry
- bitter
- indignant

160. **Ridiculous**
- absurd
- ludicrous
- preposterous

Negative Qualities
Traits/personality/character/qualities
(Supported with some synonyms)

161. Rigid (N)
- strict
- severe
- stern

162. Ruined
- bankrupt
- insolvent
- broke

163. Sadistic
- aggressive
- brutal
- cruel

164. Scheming
- devious
- calculating
- conniving

165. Scornful
- contemptuous
- disdainful
- disrespectful

166. Secretive (N)
- enigmatic
- mysterious
- reserved

167. Sedentary
- inactive
- sitting
- inert

168. Self-indulgent
- decadent
- indulgent
- hedonistic

169. Selfish
- self-centered
- egotistic
- self-interested

170. Shallow
- one-dimensional
- small-minded
- superficial

171. Shortsighted
- thoughtless
- unthinking
- restricted

172. Skeptical
- cynical
- disbelieving
- doubtful

173. Sloppy
- slack
- shoddy
- careless

174. Slow
- sluggish
- unhurried
- measured

175. Sly (N)
- crafty
- cunning
- tricky

176. Sordid
- repugnant
- dirty
- squalid

Negative Qualities
Traits/personality/character/qualities
(Supported with some synonyms)

177. **Stupid**
- unintelligent
- dim-witted
- thick

178. **Submissive**
- meek
- docile
- passive

179. **Superficial**
- phony
- fraud
- apparent

180. **Superstitious**
- irrational
- gullible
- credulous

181. **Suspicious**
- doubtful
- distrustful
- apprehensive

182. **Tactless**
- insensitive
- inconsiderate
- indiscreet

183. **Tense (N)**
- anxious
- nervous
- overwrought

184. **Thievish**
- thief-like
- stealthy
- crafty

185. **Thoughtless**
- inconsiderate
- unkind
- selfish

186. **Timid (N)**
- coy
- fearful
- nervous

187. **Treacherous**
- unfaithful
- disloyal
- deceitful

188. **Troublesome**
- wearisome
- bothersome
- upsetting

189. **Unappreciative**
- ungrateful
- showing no gratitude
- unthankful

190. **Uncaring**
- hardhearted
- callous
- heartless

191. **Uncharitable**
- unkind
- mean
- spiteful

192. **Unconvincing**
- far-fetched
- unimpressive
- not credible

Negative Qualities
Traits/personality/character/qualities
(Supported with some synonyms)

193. Uncooperative
- unhelpful
- obstinate
- disobliging

194. Uncritical
- unimaginative
- talent less
- uninspired

195. Unctuous
- groveling
- creepy
- sycophantic

196. Undisciplined
- disruptive
- disorderly
- disobedient

197. Unfriendly
- frosty
- distant
- aloof

198. Ungrateful
- thankless
- rude
- ungracious

199. Unhealthy
- damaging
- detrimental
- harmful

200. Unimaginative
- boring
- insipid
- derivative

201. Unimpressive
- unimposing
- mediocre
- average

202. Unlovable
- abhorrent
- hateful
- detestable

203. Unpolished
- unrefined
- uncultured
- unsophisticated

204. Unprincipled
- devious
- dishonest
- amoral

205. Unrealistic
- phony
- fake
- pathetic

206. Unreliable
- untrustworthy
- erratic
- undependable

207. Unrestrained
- wild
- uninhibited
- uncontrolled

208. Unstable
- Capricious
- Whimsical
- aimless

Negative Qualities
Traits/personality/character/qualities
(Supported with some synonyms)

209. **Vacuous**
- unintelligent
- stupid
- empty-headed

210. **Venomous**
- noxious
- poisonous
- deadly

211. **Weak**
- pathetic
- puny
- scrawny

212. **Zany**
- crazy
- screwy
- madcap

Neutral Qualities

When a person's qualities are neither positive or negative, we refer to them as "neutral qualities". Here we have a list with a few synonyms.

1. **Absentminded**
   - forgetful
   - distracted
   - preoccupied
   - daydreaming
2. **Amusing**
   - funny
   - humorous
   - entertaining
   - comical
3. **Artful**
   - crafty
   - devious
   - sly
   - sneaky
4. **Authoritarian**
   - strict
   - severe
   - demanding
   - controlling
5. **Businesslike**
   - professional
   - organized
   - competent
   - efficient
6. **Busy**
   - eventful
   - demanding
   - hectic
   - tiring
7. **Casual**
   - relaxed
   - informal
   - sporty
   - unceremonious
8. **Competitive**
   - spirited
   - gung ho
   - bloodthirsty
   - aggressive
9. **Complex**
   - multifaceted
   - composite
   - multipart
   - intricate
10. **Confidential**
    - secret
    - private
    - hush-hush
    - off the record
11. **Conservative**
    - traditional
    - conventional
    - conformist
    - established
12. **Contradictory**
    - opposing
    - clashing
    - conflicting
    - differing

Neutral Qualities

13. Crisp
- snappish
- brusque
- touchy
- abrupt

14. Determined
- strong-minded
- resolute
- gritty
- unwavering

15. Dominating
- controlling
- ruling
- leading
- dictating

16. Dreamy
- pensive
- vague
- faraway
- absentminded

17. Driving
- heavy
- pouring
- lashing
- powerful

18. Droll
- amusing
- funny
- comic
- witty

19. Earthy
- basic
- practical
- down-to-earth
- plain

20. Effeminate
- womanish
- niminy-piminy
- foppish
- campy

21. Emotional
- moving
- touching
- poignant
- affecting

22. Enigmatic
- mysterious
- unknowable
- inscrutable
- unfathomable

23. Experimental
- new
- untried
- investigational
- tentative

24. flabbergasted
- amazed
- astonished
- astounded
- stunned

Neutral Qualities

25. Familial
- ancestral
- household
- domestic
- marital

26. Folksy
- simple
- unaffected
- unsophisticated
- straightforward

27. Forgetful
- distracted
- inclined to forget
- preoccupied
- absentminded

28. Formal
- official
- proper
- prescribed
- recognized

29. Freewheeling
- non-interventionist
- unrestricted
- permissive
- lax

30. Hurried
- quick
- rushed
- speedy
- swift

31. Hypnotic
- mesmerizing
- spellbinding
- repetitive
- fascinating

32. Iconoclastic
- critical
- skeptical
- questioning
- doubting

33. Idiosyncratic
- personal
- individual
- distinctive
- peculiar

34. Impassive
- unemotional
- blank
- expressionless
- poker faced

35. Impersonal
- distant
- cold
- aloof
- frosty

36. Impressionable
- vulnerable
- suggestible
- susceptible
- gullible

Neutral Qualities

37. Intense
- strong
- powerful
- forceful
- passionate

38. Invisible
- imperceptible
- indistinguishable
- undetectable
- indiscernible

39. Maternal
- motherly
- caring
- tender
- gentle

40. Modern
- contemporary
- current
- up to date
- present

41. Moralistic
- moralizing
- didactic
- straitlaced
- serious

42. Mystical
- spiritual
- mystic
- numinous
- magical

43. Native
- inhabitant
- resident
- national
- local

44. Neutral
- unbiased
- impartial
- nonaligned
- disinterested

45. Noncommittal
- evasive
- vague
- ambiguous
- unrevealing

46. Ordinary
- normal
- standard
- regular
- common

47. Original
- unique
- innovative
- novel
- inventive

48. Outspoken
- frank
- candid
- open
- blunt

Neutral Qualities

49. Paternalistic
- condescending
- patronizing
- disdainful
- lofty

50. Political
- following
- supporting
- biased
- opinionated

51. Predictable
- unsurprising
- expected
- conventional
- banal

52. Preoccupied
- worried
- anxious
- inattentive
- lost in thought

53. Private
- confidential
- personal
- hush-hush
- classified

54. Proud
- conceited
- self-important
- bigheaded
- pompous

55. Questioning
- quizzical
- curious
- puzzled
- perplexed

56. Reserved
- snobbish
- standoffish
- shy
- aloof

57. Restrained
- reserved
- controlled
- self-possessed
- undemonstrative

58. Retiring
- shy
- reserved
- diffident
- introverted

59. Sarcastic
- ironic
- mocking
- sardonic
- cynical

60. Self-conscious
- awkward
- embarrassed
- ill at ease
- self-conscious

Neutral Qualities

61. Sensual
- exciting
- stirring
- tactile
- provocative

62. Solemn
- somber
- grave
- serious
- glum

63. Solitary
- private
- retiring
- introverted
- friendless

64. Stern
- severe
- harsh
- demanding
- firm

65. Strict
- severe
- stern
- stringent
- authoritarian

66. Stubborn
- obstinate
- immovable
- inflexible
- willful

67. Stylish
- fashionable
- chic
- modish
- trendy

68. Subjective
- slanted
- biased
- personal
- individual

69. Surprising
- astonishing
- astounding
- amazing
- startling

70. Soft
- yielding
- squashy
- supple
- flexible

71. Tough
- hard-hitting
- strong
- sturdy
- hard

72. Unceremonious
- abrupt
- brusque
- curt
- hasty

Neutral Qualities

73. Unchanging
- static
- fixed
- rigid
- monotonous

74. Undemanding
- easy
- straightforward
- unchallenged
- simple

75. Unfathomable
- deep
- profound
- bottomless
- unsoundly

76. Unhurried
- leisurely
- easygoing
- dawdling
- deliberate

77. Uninhibited
- not reserved
- unrestrained
- candid
- outgoing

78. Unpredictable
- random
- erratic
- changeable
- impulsive

79. Whimsical
- fanciful
- quirky
- capricious
- unusual

80. Vague
- indistinct
- unclear
- hazy
- fuzzy

81. Vindictive
- spiteful
- malicious
- bitter
- mean

82. Vulnerable
- susceptible
- defenseless
- helpless
- open to danger

83. Willful
- headstrong
- stubborn
- obstinate
- wayward

A note from the author:

Till now, we have covered almost all the important and casual usages of adjectives. Having learnt these adjectives, we should not forget using at least one adjective or a determiner prior to any noun: an abstract noun or a material noun. Even common nouns and collective nouns should be qualified with these adjectives.

A few examples to recall again:

- **A** child gets **immense great happiness** when it meets mother.
- My **great country** has given **many brawny warriors**.
- A glass of **clean, cold water** quenches the thirst of a **thirsty traveller.**
- I have **a beautiful small red bicycle.**
- **Many intelligent students** clear their **tough examinations** with the support of **a great number of unusual words** that come in English language.
- Columbus was a **adventurous and curious sailor** who travelled through **unfathomable vast oceans.**

Now, in the next chapter, you shall comprehend a small portion of grammar. This explanation shows the comparison of adjectives. The detailed understanding is in the book *Grammar Made Easy* by S. Raja

Adjective Degree Change

Adjectives are articulated in three different degrees when we compare nouns. They are Positive, Comparative and Superlative forms of adjectives.

- This food is **as sweet as** that food. (Positive degree)
- My country is **better than** your country. (Comparative degree)
- Our work is **the fastest** one. (Superlative degree)

* Formation of Comparative and Superlative

Most Adjectives of one syllable, and some of more than one, form the Comparative by adding -er and the Superlative by adding -est to the Positive.

Positive	Comparative	Superlative
Sweet	Sweeter	Sweetest
Small	Smaller	Smallest
Tall	Taller	Tallest
Bold	Bolder	Boldest
Clever	Cleverer	Cleverest
Kind	Kinder	Kindest
Young	Younger	Youngest
Great	Greater	Greatest

When the Positive ends in 'e', only -r and -st are added.

Positive	Comparative	Superlative
Brave	Braver	Bravest
Fine	Finer	Finest
White	Whiter	Whitest
Large	Larger	Largest
Able	Abler	Ablest
Noble	Nobler	Noblest
Wise	Wiser	Wisest
Fast	Faster	Fastest
Strong	Stronger	Strongest

When the Positive ends in 'y', preceded by a consonant, the 'y' is changed into 'I 'before adding -er and -est.

Positive	Comparative	Superlative
Happy	Happier	Happiest
Easy	Easier	Easiest
Heavy	Heavier	Heaviest
Merry	Merrier	Merriest
Wealthy	Wealthier	Wealthiest
Zany	Zanier	Zaniest
Scary	Scarier	Scariest

When the Positive adjective is a word of one syllable and ends in a single consonant, preceded by a short vowel, this consonant is doubled before adding -er and -est.

Positive	Comparative	Superlative
Red	Redder	Reddest
Big	Bigger	Biggest
Hot	Hotter	Hottest
Thin	Thinner	Thinnest
Sad	Sadder	Saddest
Fat	Fatter	Fattest
Wet	Wetter	Wettest

Adjectives of more than two syllables form the Comparative and Superlative by putting more and most before the Positive.

Positive	Comparative	Superlative
Beautiful	More Beautiful	Most Beautiful
Difficult	More Difficult	Most Difficult
Industrious	More Industrious	Most Industrious
Courageous	More Courageous	Most Courageous
Dangerous	More Dangerous	Most Dangerous
Extreme	More Extreme	Most Extreme
Unfathomable	More Unfathomable	Most Unfathomable
Vindictive	More Vindictive	Most Vindictive

The Royal order of Adjectives

When we use more than two adjectives, we have to follow a particular order of adjectives in a sentence. If we use two adjectives of equal altitude, we combine them by 'and'. Following is the order.

1. Observation/ feeling   lovely/beautiful/usual
2. Size   colossal/tiny/very small
3. Physical quality   clean/tidy/slim
4. Shape   round/oval/square
5. Age   ancient/new/latest
6. Colour   Pink/red/white
7. Origin   Indian/Chinese
8. Material   Gold/Glass/Wooden
9. Qualifier/ Purpose   Jogging/Running

Examples:
- I have just purchased a lovely small round latest black American glass flower vase.
- He is a smart and intelligent student.
- We enjoyed a nice long summer holidays.
- She is an interesting young woman.
- Did you enjoy delicious hot nourishing vegetable soup?

A note from the writer:
Dear reader, the detailed understanding of Adjectives, its degrees, and its royal order is well explained in forthcoming book,
The Grammar made Easy **by S. Raja**

A few Common Idiomatic Expressions & Their Meanings

1. My brother was **tickled pink** by the good news that he never expected. (To be very happy)
2. Your team was **hands down** the best team in the city. (Without competition)
3. I don't know the reason but she's been feeling pretty **down in the dumps** for a few days. (Sad or depressed)
4. The season is very bad. I'm feeling **sick as a dog**! (To be sick)
5. It seems that you are **under the weather**. Take rest. (Unwell)
6. Hey, You, **Rise and shine**! The day in over yet. (To be happy!)
7. The competition was quite tough. It was **close, but no cigar**. (Away from winning)
8. We are far from the city. We have to wait **till the cows come home**. (For a very long time)
9. Wow! This monsoon, it's raining **cats and dogs** out there! Let's enjoy it. (Very hard rain)
10. That incessant irritating sound is **driving me up the wall**! (To make annoyed)
11. This new mid-sem assignment is **a piece of cake**. (Very easy)
12. Despite his rule breaking, he was only given **a slap on the wrist.** (A mild punishment)
13. Oh! This branded T-shirt costs **an arm and a leg.** (Extremely expensive)
14. No, Don't get enraged. I was just **pulling your leg**. (Making a joke)
15. This logic is confusing. **It's Greek** to me! (Cannot understand)
16. This is not the final test. **Keep** your **chin up**. (Be happy)
17. You have a lot of time to complete the work. **Hold your horses**. (Be patient)
18. Don't worry. You are not alone, we're all **in the same boat**. (In the same position)

19. The monsoon is here. But heavy rain is a bit of **a loose cannon**. (Unpredictable)
20. He is a lazy boy. He's going to clean his room **when pigs fly**. (Impossible/ never)
21. He **turned a deaf ear** to my advice so he failed the test. (To disregard)
22. We are going to win this match **by hook or by crook** (By any means)
23. Whenever misbehavior is concerned I **put my foot down.** (To take a resolute stand)
24. Gaurangi has **made up her mind** to study in Canada. (Decided)
25. Remember, your steady work is sure to be rewarded **in the long run.** (Ultimately)
26. Mother saved her child from fire **in the nick of time**. (Just at the right moment)
27. The Covid 19 pandemic seems to have got quite **our of hand.** (Beyond control)
28. You should **hit the nail on the head** when you get a chance to solve the Problem.(to do or act the right thing)
29. The young rider, without a licence, **took to his heels** on seeing a policeman. (Ran off)
30. I visit my distant friend's home **once in a blue moon**. (Rarely)
31. **Out of the blue,** my class teacher asked a random question. (Unexpectedly, suddenly)
32. My mother **has green fingers.** You must see her flourishing kitchen Garden.(to be good at growing plants)
33. Raju was in **seventh heaven** when he published his first book. (Very happy)
34. The peon was **caught red handed** when he was about to open the principal's locker. (Caught doing a wrong act)
35. Stop preparing for the exam **at the eleventh hour.** It will not fetch good results. (At the last moment)
36. Parth decided **to burn the midnight oi**l to clear the SAT exam. (To put in a lot of effort)
37. He was jailed for ten years. Later he **turned over a new leaf** and became a good citizen. (A complete change for the betterment)

Hearty Reviews about the book...

Linda Stanton French (USA) says: *'You have a good command of the rules of English. These books are edited carefully. I hope this book is a success.'*

Sakshi Shah (A student of BCom) says: *'The first impression of this book to me was something like : All in one. Yes, it is useful for everyone. Everything can be found in this book, that is something really unique about it. I do find it perfect not only for test takers but also for people who are learning this language.*

Mukesh Raval (An educator) says: *'Sheth Sir has been teaching English for many years in my academy. His expertise in the language, and the way of teaching have influenced hundred of students. This book of Lexical Resource shall be the best tool for all the students.'*

Meshwa Soni (A First Year college student) says: *' I am a student of Sheth Sir since 2018. His creative notes have helped me a lot. Having gone through this book, I am so delighted that this shall help me in enhancing my vocabulary. The collection and compilation are awesome. I have never found a book like this.*

Ferin Patel (Std. 11) says: *'This book is a unique jewel of a kind. The content, the usefulness, and the outcome, all are very useful for a student like me. I have gathered a lot of knowledge of word power from this book. This is a successful publication.'*

Prof. NK Dave (An author of Commerce books) says: *' This book seems to be a result of hard work. Rajesh has taken much toil and trouble to support his students. This book shall allow the learners of English language in mastering new words.*

Gauri Joshi (Canada, a post graduate student) says: *'This looks very professional and very useful for all types of learners, whoever is preparing for IELTS, TOEFL or any other exam. As a student, I would like to say that this book includes every topics whichever is necessary for readers to enhance their knowledge about words. Sir, this is the perfect book for test takers. You have explained everything whatever students need to understand.'*

Nilesh Gandhi (A veteran Airforce officer) says: *'Firstly my congratulations to you for this mammoth task that you have undertaken ! I became a student again & definitely brushed up my language skills.*

Writer's Note:

Thanks for reviewing *A book of Lexical Resource* (Part 1 B1/B2 CEFR) by Rajesh Sheth (S.Raja.) More detailed references are included in Part 2 and 3. (Forthcoming soon)

Verbs, adverbs, nouns, and adjectives listed in *Grammar Made Easy,* by S. Raja, (forthcoming soon) are explained as a primary understanding of their proper usages.

This book has been thoroughly checked, however, if any wrong usage or typographical error is traced out while reading, please inform promptly.

'To err is human, to forgive is divine'

Your queries and doubts shall be solved heartily if you have any.
Feel free to mail at e-mail id: rshethsir@gmail.com

Read, understand, apply and grab the desired test score.

Rajesh Sheth (S. Raja)

Forthcoming Books Of Rajesh Sheth

Part 2: B2 Level

* Detailed understanding of:
Collocation/Paraphrasing/Redundancy and Circumlocution/Clichés/Jargon/
Ambiguity/Cohesion and Coherence/Abstract words and Concrete nouns…
and more
* List of One word for many/ Acronyms/Collocation of Verbs and Verbal
Phrases/Antonyms/Cohesive Devices/Cluttering Phrases/Connectives/Nom-
inalization of Words in a Word Family/Confusable…

Part 3: C1 Level & above

* Detailed understanding of :
Coherence and Cohesion/Structure of Sentences/Placement of Relative
Clauses/Sequence of Sentences/Avoiding Discriminatory Writing/Differ-
ence between Breathless Sentences and Clear Sentences…
* List of Idioms and Phrases/Colloquial Expressions/Quotation/Thematic
words/Linkers and Starters/Words for Personal Point of View/Idiomatic
Expression/One Word Substitute/Phobia…

My Notes:

My Notes:

Lexical Resource

My Notes:

Printed in Great Britain
by Amazon

23073975R00073